INCISION

INCISION

A Surgeon's Memoirs

Dr. Charles Douglas Adkins

Incision: A Surgeon's Memoirs

Published by Wheatmark®
610 East Delano Street, Suite 104
Tucson, Arizona 85705 U.S.A.
www.wheatmark.com

International Standard Book Number: 978-1-60494-123-4
Library of Congress Control Number: 2008927383

Front cover art by Guadalupe de la Torre.

Dedicated to

Eudora Hawkins Adkins

December 12, 1915-February 13, 2001

Contents

Book I: Father

Book II: Childhood Memories of Farm and High School

Book VI: Other Facets of my Life

Book VII: Some Later Epiphanies

C.D. Adkins, M.D.—Vitae

Undergraduate and graduate training
University of Minnesota
Internship—General Hospital, Minneapolis, Minnesota
1940-1941

Fellowship, Pathology, University of Minnesota
1941-1942

Fellowship, Anatomy, University of Minnesota
1937-1939

Preceptorship—Surgery with Dr. S.R. Maxeiner, Minneapolis, Minnesota
1942-1948

Surgical Residency VA Minneapolis (under the auspices Surgical Department, University of Minnesota July 1, 1948—July 1, 1951)

American Board—General Surgery, 1953
Clinical Instructor at the University of Minnesota, 1953-1982
American College of Surgery, 1954

Memberships:
Minneapolis Surgical Society
Minneapolis Academy of Medicine
Southern Surgical Society
Minnesota Chapter of the American College of Surgeons
Hennepin County Medical Society

American Medical Association
Foundation for Health Care Evaluation

Staff Memberships:
North Memorial Medical Center
Fairview Hospital
Fairview Southdale Hospital
Mount Sinai Hospital

Acknowledgements

Dr. Jones Adkins, my son, for reinforcement

Fred and Evelyn Brock, friends, for editing

Cheryll Ostrum, my ex-daughter-in-law, for a critique

Peggy Dior, a friend, for typing the manuscript

A special tribute goes to my friend, Leland Johnson, for his expertise in dissecting, suggesting and editing the manuscript. Without his long hours of assistance, I would not have finished.

C.D. Adkins
Green Valley, Arizona

Introduction

THIS IS A tribute to a noble aspect of the past—the country doctor. That reverent title is not extinct, however, for the following anecdotes will show the influence that such a doctor had upon his son, who through years of surgical practice, will reveal the good and bad of the medical profession. This will include some of my father's experiences and my personal remembrances of our medical careers, along with childhood memories of my life in a small town.

I was inspired and urged to record these rich experiences by my daughter, and especially by my gourmet cook and retired English teacher friend—Leland Johnson. Since time is marching on, I decided it urgent to begin recording these experiences. I will be using an anecdotal method for both my father's and my own challenging experiences.

In no way do I want to negate the overall perception of the dedication and loyalty of doctors of this day; however, in the past during the time I was intrinsically involved with medicine (1943-1982), many aspects of this profession enhanced my respect while other elements deprecated and revolted me. During those early years, almost all of the family physicians made house calls, but rarely if ever did doctors complain of the low fees. These low fees were accepted as an altruistic measure—just part of being a doctor.

During my career, I was witness to some defects within the medical profession. Some doctors, with that "greater than thou" syndrome should be exposed to a more reduced image. In the past, doctors were held in great respect; but now this has come down a notch or two, primarily because times have changed. Because of the increase in office expenses, malpractice insurance, and HMOs, less time is allotted for individual patient care. The era of the solo practitioner has been re-

placed by large group practices run by business managers and hospitals'
strict requirements. The day has long past when the individual doctor
is well acquainted with his patients and their entire family histories.
This is a contrast to the real country doctor.

Many beneficial changes have taken place since my introduction to
the medical profession in 1943; namely antibiotics, vaccines, such as
those for Polio in 1955, improved and expedited chemical tests, radiol-
ogy imaging, and increasing specialization in all fields. The last change
has given rise to microsurgery, necessary for limb attachment, refined
eye, brain and cardiovascular surgery. Joint replacement, laparoscopic
and same day surgery are extremely important innovations.

Other changes include: (1) early hospital ambulation (2) organ
transplantation and stem cell research including robot surgery (3) closure of tuberculosis sanatoriums with almost complete obliteration of
communicable diseases (4) recognition of the carcinogenic effects of
tobacco (5) establishment of Medicare and (6) pharmacological drugs
for mental illness and hypertension (7) emphasis on a balanced diet
and exercise (8) recognition of the HIV virus (9) utilization of PSA
for detection for prostatic cancer (10) less radical surgery for breast
cancer (11) the recognition of deoxyribonucleic acid (DNA) (12) the
electronic microscope (13) refined blood typing and screening of blood
products for transfusion (14) paramedics' initial care at the emergency
site (15) helicopter transfer (16) innovated methods to assist the dia-
betic patient in self-management (17) establishment of trauma, burn
and shock centers (18) and, of extreme value, the establishment of hospice and chemotherapy. While any one of the above has not reduced
health care costs, each has decreased morbidity and mortality. Excessive
malpractice awards are the downside.

Hospitals have improved by departmentalizing patient care; such
as, intensive care, cardiovascular, orthopedic, and pediatric units. In
order to be accredited, hospitals must meet strict standards; therefore,
they are audited and graded every two to three years. Now, surgical
privileges are granted only after strict requirements are met. Within
the hospital staff, each department has a committee with a chief; consequently, each physician has to meet the existing standards of his/
her specialty. If not, the doctor may be requested to appear before the

respective committee. American board recertification is necessary after ten years of practice.

Another dramatic change has been the increase in women graduates from about 5% in 1942 to over 50% at the present time; for instance, the 2004 matriculation class at the University of Minnesota had 143 women and 142 men.

BOOK I

Father

You can love completely without complete understanding.

A River Runs Through It—Norman Maclean

Dad's Early Life

ONE OF THE real country doctors was C. M. Adkins, who was born in 1870 in Wayne County in the hills of West Virginia. His father, an austere, stern, black haired, cold-natured man named Peter Adkins, married a Caylor, a petite brown-eyed woman who loved to smoke a corncob pipe. Before taking a puff she would sit by a window, so if a visitor passed by she could quietly hide the pipe under her apron. We found nothing embarrassing about her habit because at Christmas time, we would replenish her tobacco cache.

Since Wayne County was situated in a Gray Zone after the Civil War, bitter feelings were rampant among its citizens. To avoid the animosity, the Adkins and the Caylor families, along with others, traveled by covered wagon to Minnesota. Since Peter had served in the Union Army as a scout, he utilized his knowledge to guide the wagon trains.` They would stop on weekends for religious services. Because of their loud singing, they were called the Howling Presbyterians. Many of them settled near Kimball, in central Minnesota, where they took up farming. My father, the eldest of five children, was a hard-working young man who had very little time for frivolity, although he would on occasion play baseball on the Fourth of July or at other festive occasions. His signature was "All Work And No Play." During those farm days, he was inspired to become a physician through his acquaintance with Kimball's lone family doctor. He had little money, so as a young man he left the farm along with this suppressed desire. To obtain expenses he became a schoolteacher and later a telegraph operator.

He met his first unusual challenge when he accepted a teaching position where his rigid, determined personality was manifested. It was in a small town farming community somewhere in North Dakota. The students were very poorly disciplined, and no teacher returned because of their unruly behavior. They, instead of the teacher, had control. The students' ages, interestingly, were from eight to 18. To torment the teacher, they would lock him out of the schoolhouse, then dance and play games. One day, when my father came to school and found the door locked, he picked up a cord wood log and knocked the door open. He then grabbed the boy whom he perceived to be the ringleader (aged 17 or 18). He threw him to the floor, picked him up again, knocked him down, and picked him up again. Finally, he thrust him into a seat and said, "You be here in the morning, have the fire going, the wood box filled, and the floor swept." He told him he knew he was bright and could excel in class even though he was only in second grade. When my dad told me this story, he admitted to being fearful that the boys would gang up on him.

Unexpectedly, the next morning the recalcitrant boy was on time, the school was swept clean, the fire was going, and the wood box was full. By the end of that year, the student had excelled in class, jumping to the sixth grade, solely because of his teacher's discipline. One of my father's innovations was to make the students read a sentence backwards, and then forwards, then backwards again—a unique method of teaching reading. Some parents tried to influence my father to stay because of his success.

To obtain better financial support for his medical school, he accepted a position as a telegraph operator. At this time, he shared living quarters with a bachelor friend. He never related much about that premedical experience except that they rarely washed their plates—just wiped them with a slice of bread and then turned them over in order to keep off the flies. He chuckled, however, when he told me of an incident in his life as a telegraph operator. His partner was going around sniffing the very foul air in search of the source. "Probably a dead rat or mouse," my dad said. "I passed a little gas. Do you suppose that's it?" His friend was so rebuffed that their friendship became shaded.

Following the two brief careers of teaching and working in the telegraph office, he volunteered for service in the Army. Prior to embarking to the Philippines, a gambler friend offered my father a proposition: "If you join me, I will guarantee you a yearly profit of fifteen to twenty thousand dollars. I need you as a partner to control my money because otherwise I'll spend it." Dad then asked him how they would accomplish this. His answer was: "I can wiggle ourselves out of the

Army." Dad rejected the proposition. During off hours the spurned gambler would sit and deal cards with just either his right or left hand.

My father's early goal, however, was interrupted by volunteering in the Spanish-American War in 1898. While in the Philippines, he had an unusual experience. The engineering department was having problems keeping corner telephone poles erect. Even though my Dad was only a corporal, his farm chores of putting in fence posts enabled him to solve the problem.

While he didn't talk much about any of his experiences, he did relate one frightening incident involving troops that were called in to clean up a village. When an unattended squad was working, a whistle signal sounded. The local peasants immediately drew their machetes and massacred the entire squad. In revenge, the company was ordered to move into the village and kill everything that moved: men, women, children and even dogs. Sometimes later, he himself was involved in a similar incident even though he only killed dogs.

As an excellent horseman and pistol marksman, he would ride into the village where some of the ubiquitous dogs would run out and bark at the horse's heels. Somehow, he communicated to the owners to keep the dogs at bay or suffer the consequences. Shortly thereafter, he demonstrated his threat when five barking dogs suffered fatal wounds as he galloped by.

While there was little time for social relationships, the cultural difference kept the soldiers' romantic desires at bay. One of the best presents a suitor could offer a girl was a handful of baked or grilled grasshoppers.

Following his discharge, he went to Kansas City where he seriously pursued his MD degree. One of his professors was Dr. Arthur Hertzler, the famous surgeon and author of *The Horse and Buggy Doctor*, as well as many surgical books. Dad had great reverence for the outspoken and industrious Dr. Hertzler. One example demonstrates both traits: he innovated total thyroidectomy for hyperthyroidism, basing this operation and decision on his long follow-up experience of patients with partial thyroidectomy (sub-total). Often these patients would return years later with heart failure due to chronic hyperthyroidism. When he presented a paper on the subject to a prestigious eastern American college meeting, he was asked in the post question/answer session; "How do you prevent injury to the recurrent laryngeal nerves?" Dr. Hertzler retorted, "If you don't know how to do that, you don't belong in the operating room." The college never requested further papers.

In the late nineteenth and twentieth centuries, there were no American centers for surgical training; therefore, some doctors studied in Germany and Austria. Dad told me Hertzler studied one year in Germany, during which time he took only one day off. Dr. Hertzler's cancellation of a visit to our home in Thief River Falls in Minnesota was a deep disappointment.

Dad demonstrated self-confidence and initiative. After graduation, he purchased a small leather kit that contained a surgical knife and forceps. He stopped at the hospital in order to watch a tonsillectomy being performed by one of his teachers, who happened to be the most successful Eye, Ear, Nose & Throat doctor in Kansas City. While standing by the operating table, Dad noticed the child had become cyanotic (lack of oxygen). My dad immediately recognized the lethal consequences; and while the surgeon was helplessly standing by, Dad without hesitation, seized the forceps from his kit, reached over the operating table, grasped the tongue, and pulled it forward, thus clearing the airway and saving the child's life.

Until the past thirty-two years, tonsillectomy was a common procedure. In no way would it meet present day indications. Adults were operated under local and children under ether anesthesia. Severe deep ether anesthesia produces complete muscle relaxation; thus the child's tongue, in the above case, receded and blocked the airway. Apparently, no tongue depressor was used. After finishing the tonsillectomy, the surgeon looked at my father and said, "I want to see you in the next room." While waiting for the interview, Dad told me he was very fearful of being severely reprimanded. Instead of a censure, the doctor said, "Charlie, I need you. I have the largest practice in Kansas City, but at times under rare critical conditions, I panic. If you will join me, I will make you my full partner."

This offer was his second potentially lucrative refusal. Instead of accepting the prestigious position, he married Minnie Hill, a beautiful eighteen-year-old girl, took his young bride to a small town near an Indian Reservation in central Minnesota, and opened a private practice there. Apparently, he was captivated by the flowing well in Ogema, where he practiced diligently in this pristine place for several years.

It was here where my brother Galen and sister Arda were born. My youngest brother, Jack, and I were born later in Grygla.

In spite of loyalty and admiration for my father, there remain a few shadows about his disciplinary nature. When we lived in Grygla, I always felt that it was unjust and without cause to have bedtime punctually set at eight o'clock. Laughed at by the other kids because of our curtailed playing time, we were angry and fretful prior to sleep. He was very strict about this edict. At age eight while I was playing at my future wife's home, the phone rang, "It's your dad; come home immediately." I then realized it was past bedtime and with marked trepidation, I ran home. Doing so, I tripped over a small wagon in the neighbor's yard. I started to cry, not because I was hurt, but because of fear. Dad was waiting for me. He asked, "Why are you crying?" I told him I had stumbled over a wagon, and he responded, "It's past your bed time; now I am going to give you something you can cry about." It was a whip lashing. Yes, I did cry. At that moment, I felt dislike and alienation. Whenever we followed a question put to him with "Why?" his answer was, "Because I said so."

A few years later, another severe beating took place. I was assigned a job to nail all the outside warped boards on our house (several paint applications would have prevented that). I was instructed to take the hammer over to Viking's Blacksmith Shop to get a broken handle replacement. While on the way, I found a good hand pump hose. At that point, a Model T touring car came by. Thinking that it may be useful, I picked up the hose and tossed it towards the back seat. A bit later, the farmer and my dad approached me. The farmer told my dad that I had thrown it directly at him. Without allowing me an explanation, I was beaten severely with the hose. During the punishment, he accused me of being upset because I had to nail down the boards. Unfortunately, the brass coupling was at the end of the hose.

Crying and on my hands and knees, I crawled to the house. Knowing that I had meant no harm, I experienced not only physical but emotional pain. After my sobs relented, I had a strong urge to run away, but I had no place to go. While it took some time for the welts and bruises to disappear, the emotional imprint never did. Years later, I confronted Dad and told my factual story. He said, "Why didn't you tell me? I would have kicked the shit out of the farmer." I told him feeble attempts to do so were ignored. Nothing more was ever said.

He was very Spartan in nature. We were often told, "Stand up like a man; don't cry." In practice, he himself never cried. His discipline was manifested one time during the annual exciting Pennington County Fair in Thief River Falls. Since my brothers and I were anxious to attend, he consented to our request. Along with a few dollars, came the qualification that we could go Saturday if we finished haying the front forty acres and be back to work on the following Sunday morning. With much effort, we finished the field, but we didn't get back from the fair until near dawn. We were late because Galen graciously helped a family with car trouble, driving them forty miles out of our way. With little or no sleep, we went back to work Sunday morning.

Paradoxically, I don't remember my brother Jack ever-receiving harsh punishment. He had Dad's brown eyes, black hair, and his cussing vocabulary. Swearing was well illustrated in an incident related to me by my mother-in-law, Lilly Hawkins. When she observed Jack playing near the sidewalk, she smiled and said "Hello, Jack." "Shut up you son-of-a-bitch," came the retort from the five year old boy. He knew the words but not the meaning. While Lilly was very upset, she didn't tell Dad. If he had known, I wonder what his reaction would have been: to punish or to be amused by an extension of himself.

His Daughter, Arda

I never dared question Dad's judgment. However, his harsh and cruel treatment of my sister Arda was unforgivable. After mother died and our Grygla housekeeper had left, Arda assumed the head of the household. In the summer, she would cook and bring food out to us in the field. Jack and I had the dishwashing role. Since we used bar soap that didn't cut the grease, it seemed that a rim of grease was always left on the side of the dishpan. Arda frequently asked us to wash stacked up pantry pans that we would leave to soak. She also made excellent candy, especially divinity.

Invariable, Dad was at the hospital, so the only one to discipline our table manners was our sister. Since none of us had any knowledge of etiquette, we made our own rules. Instead of politely passing the bread, Galen became an expert at tossing the slices like a Frisbee; in fact, after practicing, we all became experts.

Not only did I learn how to toss bread properly according to my older brother's instruction, but I accurately threw a handful of molten butter onto the cropped head of my kid brother Jack. While angrily cussing me, he grabbed the butter and threw it back at me. Missing the target, it splashed onto the wall of the dining room where it left a large grease spot in the wallpaper. My father apparently didn't notice it so the episode was never brought up.

While Arda was very intelligent and musical, she had a wild side. Dad allowed her to drive forty miles to Thief River Falls for piano lessons in which she progressed rapidly. When as a teenager, she started to "run out," Dad sent her to a Catholic school in Grand Forks, North Dakota, for her remaining two years of high school. She was expelled because of failure to obey their strict dormitory rules. This so angered my father that he took her to the train in Thief River Falls and sent her off with fifty dollars. She ended up in Chicago as a bewildered young girl. She never spoke about it, nor did we ask. In essence, she just vanished. There was no correspondence. Then four or five years later, she showed up at our home in Thief River Falls with no explanation of her activities other than she had been living in Chicago.

Her later years were even more bizarre. She married a farmer and lived about twenty miles from Thief River Falls. The marriage disintegrated because of her abnormal behavior. While her husband loved her, and was very understanding, he agreed that a mental institution was imperative. She was admitted to the mental hospital in Fergus Falls, Minnesota, where she became incorrigible. A decision was made to give her a frontal lobotomy. Later, when proper medications were available, she became manageable, wrote poetry, played the piano and even married another member at the rest home. Her remaining years were spent in rest homes. When Eudora and I visited her, she would introduce us to her numerous friends, never forgetting their names and often singing and playing without notes. Finally, she succumbed to a brain tumor. After her admission to the Fergus Falls' mental institution, Dad never visited her again. When she was young and talked about becoming a doctor, my father squashed the idea of women doctors.

Dad's Idiosyncrasies

Dad was adamant against cigarette smoking; paradoxically, he was profoundly addicted to nicotine via the copious chewing of his favorite tobacco, Redman. The only time that he was without a chew was while he was eating, sleeping or during surgery in the operating room. The doctors at Mercy Hospital at Thief River Falls simply put the sterile gowns over their undershirts and street pants. Dressed thus, one day I observed him reach into his right rear pocket and extract an abundant amount of tobacco, just as the dressing had been applied.

Obviously, tobacco chewing necessitates expectoration. While in the office, he utilized the adjacent sink; when he was reading his journals at home, he used a nearby empty Hills' Brothers coffee can. When he was driving his Model T, he aimed at the floor space adjacent to the high gear lever so the juice would hit the ground. Since the space just to the left of the steering column was small, loss of aim left small tobacco mounds on the floorboard. If the door window was down, however, he would use that open space. After he bought a Model A Ford, Jack and I had to duck down and to the right in order to avoid the blast of juice. Just as he started to roll down the window, one of us would give a Paul Revere warning, "Duck down, tobacco juice is coming!" The back left side of upholstery forever had a deep burnt sienna stain. In the cold wintry days, he kept an empty can on the floorboard. At Christmas, we contributed to the problem. There were no gift questions; we just replaced his Redman supply.

My father's intransigent personality prevented anyone from influencing his decisions or opinions. A family practitioner related two episodes that occurred when he was practicing in Thief River Falls. The head nurse, who was also the Mercy Hospital administrator, was immensely disliked by the nurses and doctors. The hospital board of directors called a meeting in order to discuss the situation and arrive at a decision. Each member was asked to present a solution. By the time it came to Dr. Adkins, enjoying his chew of tobacco and quietly listening to the discussion, no decision had been reached. So they asked for his opinion. The meeting disbursed after he said, "Fire the son-of-a-bitch."

The same doctor related another incident. I was always cognizant that Dad disliked Dr. Ed Bratrud, a Thief River Falls family practitioner, whose practice was so large that he built his own private hospital. The story-telling physician was at that time working for Dr. Bratrud; but on this day, he was watching my father perform an autopsy (Dad was the county coroner). When he was sawing open the skull, some brain tissue bulged out. At that moment Dad scoped up the brain tissue with his hand and said, "More damn brains here than in that Bratrud outfit." Silence ruled throughout the remaining autopsy.

Our father was extremely self-reliant, a bit opinionated and a non-conformist. He had no accolades for dentists, ministers, undertakers, insurance administrators, or politicians. He also scoffed at people whom he called "uppity," those who stood on protocol and whose behavior was always circumspect. His apparel demonstrated his attitude. He could care less if his pants were un-pressed or tobacco stained, or if there were a blatant un-matching of his shirt and tie. Rarely did he really "dress up." I don't remember his second wife Alice or his ever taking either one of his two suits to the cleaners.

There was one time, however, when Dad got his comeuppance. The hospital electricity was supplied by multiple storage batteries which covered an entire wall. The dynamo needed to be started by an adjacent engine. My father usually did this by himself. On one occasion, however, the engine refused to start. Therefore, he called upon Phil Hawkins, Eudora's father, who was a master machinist. As soon as the mechanic arrived, Dad started to give him instructions. That's when Phil grabbed his tools and said, "To hell with you. I'm leaving. Start the engine yourself." Unlike my father's nature, he hurriedly asked him to stay.

On two occasions Dad unknowingly but sheepishly embarrassed me. One hot summer day I accompanied him to a medical meeting in Crookston, Minnesota. Actually, on this occasion, he was dressed up but with a screamingly loud, hideous green shirt and un-matching tie. While listening to a paper being presented by the Mayo Clinic Chief of Neurosurgery, Dad stood up (we sat in the front row) and while taking off his coat, thus displaying his colors, he said, "Goddamn it's hot in here." Immediately most of the other attending doctors (including me) shed their coats. I felt triumphant and proud of his unilateral action, but inwardly I was embarrassed about his noticeable attire.

Another embarrassment was on Dads' Day, when he came to a University of Minnesota Gophers' football game. That evening as he dined in the frat house, he was in a jolly and loquacious mood. While eating, however, he took out his false teeth, licked off the food particles from the mold, replaced them, and continued talking. While I felt uneasy, my frat brothers were listening so intently they didn't seem to notice.

After all, they were medical students. If cadavers didn't faze them, why should the simple process of cleaning false teeth upset them?

I had suspected that my father was having an affair with his long-term office nurse, who was very devoted to him. She performed as his ether anesthetist, his office nurse and laboratory technician. He once told me she had repulsive halitosis that he solved by local gum application of an iodine solution. On several occasions, my suspicions of the affair were aroused. Once when I entered the empty office, I heard from the next room what sounded like pants being rearranged or pulled up. Soon, thereafter, she appeared standing flushed and silent by the microscope. She expressed unusually deep remorse at Dad's military funeral.

We were always under Dad's jurisdiction. One of his dogmatic idiosyncrasies was counterproductive. Since extracurricular reading was limited, I would ask Dad the meaning of words. Because it was obvious his sons' vocabularies were poor, he made Jack and me start learning five words a day, starting on page one of the Webster's Unabridged Dictionary. He advised us that if one knows all of the words in that dictionary, college wouldn't be necessary. The dictionary assignments only lasted a few weeks. Book reading assignments would have been more beneficial.

My father always wanted to be in control. In later years, he became somewhat contemptuous as evidenced by several incidents. In the early sixties, he developed diabetes, resulting in a complication of a large right thigh abscess at the site of insulin injections. Concerned, my stepmother called me and asked me to come home from Minneapolis. Incision drainage was necessary. When I started to do so under local anesthetic, he barked at me to stop. I convinced him surgical and hospital care was mandatory.

He subsequently consented to hospitalization at the University of Minnesota under the care of the much-admired Dr. O. H. Wangensteen. He was taken to the hospital by a local hearse (at that time used as ambulances). On the way, he complained of the slow speed and urged the driver to increase the speedometer level. While there, my previous classmate Dr. John Lewis, who at the time was chief resident, drained the abscess through an extensive incision. My father never mentioned Dr. Wangensteen, and I doubt that he ever saw or visited him. On the day of discharge, I was reprimanded because he had to wait for me.

He was pacified after I told him of important surgical duties. While he was being wheeled down the corridor, not one nurse smiled or said goodbye.

As soon as he was settled in our Minneapolis home, I was ordered to remove the bandage and told, "Tape that damn thing shut." I did so with some trepidation (the incision rapidly healed with no further problems). His next order to my wife Eudora was to buy and cook some brains. He was anemic, pale and weak; I transfused him with my brother Jack's blood. Surprisingly, he did not object.

Dr. C.M. Adkins' boyhood home in Kimball, Minnesota. From left: unidentified, father, mother, Dr. Adkins

Another Side of Dad

My FATHER, IN spite of his serious manner, did have a sense of humor. He would frequently joke with his patients. One morning the nurses asked, "Anything new happen last night?"

"Yes, last night a baby was born without a penis."

"Oh my God, what's going to happen?"

"When she becomes eighteen, most likely one will be inserted."

Dad, however, did not like any jokes played on him. This was revealed by an incident on April's Fool day, when my kid brother and I tried a joke on him. We had planned a trip to Thief River Falls, forty miles away, so it was necessary to have the Model T in ship-shape condition. Jack and I went in and told Dad that the car had a flat tire. He didn't seem disturbed or annoyed. Instead of an expression of disappointment, he simply responded with a chuckle. "Is that so?" We were the deflated ones.

Nor was Dad a person of idle chatter. On an occasion such as Thanksgiving, we would visit our cousins the sweet and kind Aunt Dora and her husband, Delles. What "ambrosia"—turkey, beef roast, sweet potatoes with marshmallows, mashed potatoes and gravy, cranberry sauce, fresh succulent buns and homemade ice cream (we took turns at the churn). These festivities were cut short with his curt, "Time to go home." The town of Trail was fifty miles away from Grygla.

Another holiday was usually spent with Dora, his kid sister. The Fourth of July before and after would be celebrated by lighting firecrackers, the more potent the better. We would put them under a tin can or a bottle and watch the bottle shatter or the ascension of the can. Once my kid brother, Jack, suffered a gash under his left eye when a bottle exploded—a near disaster. At home in Grygla the Fourth of July evening was spent in the front yard with Dad's lighting sparklers and

Roman candles. Another out of town trip of exultation was to the Red Lake Narrows Indian Reservation, taken infrequently, because travel was slowed due to the poor road. Most passages had to be made over corduroy (multiple poplar or other tree trunks placed side by side) that traversed over low areas. The car then slowly bumped forward. Our day would be spent swimming or playing on the beautiful sandy beaches that frequently had beached logs left over from old logging days. In later years, Indians forbad white men to enter the Reservation. On these occasions Dad was more amenable than demanding.

Dad would often take personal risks to help others in stress. In a conversation with my father about the intricacies and ethics of medical practice, I asked him this question about his practice in Ogema: "Dad did you ever do an abortion?" He said, "Doug, there was an occasion when that term could have applied. A beautiful 18-year-old girl, the daughter of the mercantile storeowner came into my office. Fearing she was pregnant because her menstrual period was overdue, she said, "If I am definitely pregnant, I am going to commit suicide." In that locality resided a so-called Lochinvar, who was a ladies' man. He preyed on young women, some virgins and some not, promising marriage in order to obtain sex. Following his interval of satisfaction, he would release his victim and seek another conquest. This young lady fell victim to his rhetoric, ignoring her plea to marry. My father, who was impressed with her character, said, "Let me check you to see." He then put her up into stirrups on the examining table and with sterile technique inserted a small probe into the cervix. He told her he didn't think she was pregnant. Indeed, all went well and no suicide occurred. He told me that there was no question in his mind about her sincerity. While he did not come right out and say he had done an abortion, I have the feeling that he had. He made this decision to save a young girl's life. He wanted to prevent her from committing suicide or seeking out a back alley abortionist to probably die from sepsis (there is a sequel). At that time, if a doctor was proven to have done an abortion, his license would have been taken away.

He also was self righteous and moralistic. Since contraceptive measures were not used in the early 1900's, large families prevailed. The women were burdened with household duties: cooking, washing, churning, childcare, sewing and at times farm work. He was cognizant of the devastating effect that this burden took on some women. If such an individual came to him and it was apparent that pre-maturing aging and failing health were occurring, and especially if there was the slightest complaint of abdominal discomfort, she would be advised to have surgery because of "chronic appendicitis." He would then tie her tubes and also remove her appendix. He would say that he had found a certain female condition which most likely would prevent any addition to her already large family. He related to me, "Having one kid after another is destroying them." He made no apology. Obviously, he didn't do it for remuneration in view of the fact that payments were few and far between.

Such incidents were infrequent. After he told me about some isolated cases, I vividly remember an individual who would have benefited from tubal ligation. Once when I accompanied him on a collecting trip, a very haggard, graying farm wife appeared at the door (kids' noises from within). She was vaguely familiar. I was shocked, recalling she had attended Crookston Agricultural School with me about fifteen years earlier. She showed no signs of recognition. I couldn't remove her image from my mind. It seemed incredible that a person could have aged so quickly. Needless to say, no payment was received on that collecting trip.

As with all doctors, sometimes instant life-saving decisions had to be made. While there were vaccinations for small pox, no immune injections existed for diphtheria, a dreadful infection that produced swelling and suffocating casts in the respiratory system. He related to me that he once responded to an emergency call about a young boy who had advanced and increasing respiratory distress. On arrival, Dad recognized that death was imminent because the boy was cyanotic and barely gasping. He said, "I quickly grabbed the child, put him on my right knee and told the nurse to hand me my scalpel. I didn't have time to switch the boy to my left knee. Then, using my left hand, I cut down and opened his trachea, and with the forceps withdrew the air-stopping membrane." Breathing was restored. The nurse stayed with the boy for twenty-four hours or more, keeping the airway open by repeatedly utilizing the grasping forceps. My question to Dad was, "How did you keep the trachea open?" "Very simple" he replied, "I placed a suture through one side of the open trachea, muscle, and skin while another similar stitch was placed on the other side. Then by tying the two sutures together at the back of the neck, <u>patency </u>(keeping the airway open) was assured. To me it was innovative, ingenious and admirable. For him, it was apparently his duty, just part of a day's work. Indeed, a young life saved by a country doctor! He didn't comment to me about the parents' gratefulness.

Except for my father's use of tooth extractor pliers, he used tools in only two other instances. Once I observed him do delicate work with a power saw. At one o'clock in the morning I was summoned to his office. On entering I was flabbergasted by the scenario. There sat the town's ladies' man holding his immensely swollen penis with a brass coupling at its base. Apparently he had used the device to retain his erection and to enhance the sensation. At the end of the act he was unable to remove the brass ring.

In front of him sat my father with a grin on his face and an electric saw in his hands. He proceeded to first cut through the dorsal side of the coupling and then by lifting the penis, severed the vertical side. In the midst of the cutting, the saw skidded over the skin of the appendage with no damage. Thus freed, the patient paid my father $35 and went sheepishly into the night.

This incident demonstrated unique serendipity. Without removal of the ring, the man would have lost his penis to gangrene. I'm certain my father was the only doctor in town who owned a saw. Had the patient not sought out my father, the errant lover's romantic life would have ended. Dad left the two pieces of brass on top of his roll top desk as a humorous reminder of the enormous diversities a country doctor is called upon to solve.

Another instance which brought a humorous result from the use of tools involved an animal. Dad scoffed at the idea of sheep shearing as being difficult. To prove his point, he attempted the procedure on a wooly ewe. After wrestling with the sheep for almost an hour, he released the poor animal with multiple skin injuries and tufts of wool still on the body.

Challenges and Responsibilities

IN THIS SMALL town of Grygla, he was forced to assume other responsibilities. While walking by a nearby culvert, a man was struck by lightning, the bolt entering the body near his right ear and exiting from his left foot. The body was placed in our garage, and there Dad showed my brother Galen how to embalm a body, first by releasing the blood via a cut down on a femoral vein, followed by embalming fluid forcibly injected into the adjacent femoral artery. I stood by as an awed and interested spectator, again admiring my father's ability.

The treatment and survival of a severe head injury case still amazes me. Prompt and expertise care in a country hospital with only skylight and electric bulbs for visualization during pre-antibiotic therapy bears emphasis. Once, when I was visiting him in his Thief River Falls office, he introduced me to an old-time patient; and as he was showing me the long, nearly faded scalp scar, he related the story. While this man was disking a plowed field, his horses bolted, throwing him onto the fresh earth. One of the disks severed a flap of scalp and skull. Dad had to remove gobs of dirt and grass and even a small portion of brain tissue. He emphasized the copious sterile water irrigation, after which he re-sutured the flap. Fortunately, there was only a minimal amount of residual arm muscle impairment—another triumph for a competent, self-confident country doctor.

After Dad left Grygla and moved to Thief River Falls, another incident demonstrated his inherent ability. During a grouse-hunting trip, a local Thief River Falls physician was inadvertently shot in his right lower leg by a physician friend. The family refused my dad's plea to allow him to carry out an initial debridement. Instead, they decided to wait until the doctor's MD brother arrived from North Dakota. After the prolonged delay, the decision was made to transfer him to the Minnesota University Hospital. He returned home with a below-the-knee amputation. Dad repeatedly told me, "I know damn well I could have saved that leg." I believed him. He was no braggart, just self-confident.

Family doctors not only administered the care of emergencies such as cuts, bruises, fractures, pediatric problems, pregnancies and skin disorders they also accepted personal emotional problems. My dad told me a story about a woman in her late thirties who confided in him that her life, even though she was actively engaged in social activities, seemed empty. She was known in the neighborhood for her immaculate dress, being active in all of the social functions. Then instead of being outgoing and gregarious, she seemed withdrawn. My father knew that she appeared happily married; he was also aware that they were childless. My dad advised, "Go home and get pregnant." To emphasize the success of his resolution, he told me that months after the birth of her baby, he saw her standing out in the yard hanging up baby clothes. As she happily shouted, "Hi Doc," he noticed that she was wearing an apron over a comely dress. What, no antidepressant medication, no repeated couch consultation? They were not invented then. Just simple advice by a country doctor.

Although at times, he was penurious, he never displayed any wanting for valuable possessions. I was aware of only three properties he truly valued: an 1898 12-gauge shotgun and an antique clock that was completely constructed of wood except for the chains and weights for the mechanism. The clock is an Adkins' family heirloom that is passed down from generation to generation to the eldest son. Dad received it from his father, my brother Galen got it from Dad, and now Galen's son, Galen, Jr., (a retired veterinarian) has possession. Dad also prized his beautifully inscribed gold snap up cover watch. This was given to me but sadly, it was one of the valuable items stolen when thieves broke into my Minneapolis condo. In addition, Dad later succumbed to his desire and bought a new luxurious Packard (I don't recall any tobacco spitting episodes in that car).

Of utmost importance was to bring Grygla good hospitalization. In this small town, he built a community hospital, utilizing his own funds and stock sales. For its time, it was exceptionally well equipped. It was located about forty yards from our house, which stood on a parcel of twenty acres. The hospital was a two-story building with a big basement, two underground cement rainwater reservoirs, and two large front porches. Sewage was disposed via a long draining trench that transcended to the river about four hundred yards away. The well, pump, laundry, dynamo and multiple storage batteries were housed nearby. The barn, garage and icehouse were also close. The top floor of the hospital was partitioned into individual patient rooms, one small ward and an operating room that had a large skylight above the operating table. An adjacent portion was utilized for hand washing and instrument sterilizing.

The first floor had rooms for the nurses, a large kitchen, a bathroom (with a tub), an x-ray room, dad's office, a big waiting room, and a room that intrigued me: his apothecary and laboratory. Bottles of medicine lined the shelves. A microscope and delicate armed apothecary scale were of special interest. The scale was a hands-off item because it was intrinsically delicate, able to accurately weigh milligram units of medicinal powder. A cabinet contained several plier-type forceps (utilized for tooth extraction), measuring glasses, and various size syringes. Other items had their place, such as the dental chair, used for examinations and tooth extractions, and a thick glass plate on which he mixed salves with a palate knife.

A large x-ray machine with a bell-shaped electrode tube was in the room across from the apothecary. Depending on the origin, olfactory senses would be awakened by various odors: pungent smell of ozone after an x-ray, a nauseating one following the drainage of an abdominal abscess, a manure odor in the waiting room from farmers' shoes, and always the pleasant medicinal scent from the laboratory. Ether was the only choice of general anesthesia, thus it was always present following surgery. Of course, the kitchen always expelled its gustatory flavors. When x-rays were taken, one could hear the buzzing from the sparking x-ray tube. Since the machine required much voltage, it was mandatory to have all outlets turned off. X-rays were mainly used for bone and chest examinations with smoked glass plates used as film. After an x-ray was taken, the adjacent area was filled with ozone odor. My father also did fluoroscopic examinations. It was not uncommon for some doctors to receive x-ray burns on their hands unless they had protected themselves with lead impregnated gloves.

Wrist fractures were common during the Model T era because

cranking the engine was precarious. If the engine backfired, the crank would snap counterclockwise; and if a thumb were incorrectly placed on the handle, enough energy would cause painful fractures. Ford tractors were also one of the culprits.

As I remember, the hospital corridors always seemed to be quiet except for the discordant symphony of clanking kitchen pans, soft laughter from the nurses, and coughing and sneezing from patients in the waiting room. At an early age, I spent much time in the hospital. Unusual memories remain.

Dad used his strength to what he would call the patient's advantage. When Pa, as we always called him, was doing a difficult tooth extraction, yes- there was an occasional grunt of pain. The patient's head would be firmly held with one of his arms, while the other arm wriggled and pulled. Out would come the tooth. It was then held up in front of the patient as if it were a trophy or door prize. Occasionally, there was quite a struggle with Dad's inserting considerable energy on the squirming victim. He once extracted twenty teeth in one day at one dollar per tooth. During the winter, there was a magenta snow trail of expectorant all the way from the hospital to the downtown street. Even though Dad rarely castigated the medical profession, he once told me that dentists did not know anything about sterile technique nor did they know how to pull teeth. He explained to me that it was necessary to wiggle the tooth, then pull. He learned that technique as youth on the farm from pulling out deteriorated fence posts. Paradoxically, he failed his children by not advising prophylactic dental care or dental visits. We all had severe dental problems, and he had false teeth in his early fifties.

I also remember seeing patients who just left his hospital office with bandages or plaster casts that had been applied after suture lacerations or a fracture. He would dispense his own medicine and mix the salves on a thick glass plate. One day I watched him mix some salve, which he then smeared over thin webbed gauze. When this cool application was applied to the burned leg of a young girl, her reply was, "That feels so good."

In addition to tooth pulling and setting fractures, my father dealt with hearing and breathing problems. During fall threshing time, the air around the threshing rigs was extremely dusty. One season a farmer came to the office complaining of hearing impairment. With little or no interrogation, Dad simply went over and filled a large metal syringe with warm water. He had the patient hold a banana shaped pan against his face. While he pulled up the ear, warm water was forced into the external canal. Gobs of dirty water and dust particles were flushed from both ears. Hearing was restored, the satisfied farmer paid and left. I was amazed. One spring day, a father brought in his young son, who had pushed a pussy willow into one nostril. I watched as dad told the boy to take a deep breath, close the other nostril while pressing a finger against it and blow hard. When he did so, the foreign object flew out. I looked up and thought how absolutely astonishing.

Amidst all the observing of my father's work, occasionally, I was allowed to eat in the kitchen with the nurses, janitor and patients. At one meal, an elderly woman who was sitting just across from me, with trembling hands, attempted to bring grapes to her mouth. She tried to transport the grapes, and in doing so, they would repeatedly fall off the spoon. For some reason, it upset me. For years, I could not eat canned grapes. (Now as a nonagenarian, I have similar non-Parkinson's tremor and consequently I have great empathy for her).

Dr. Adkins (center in sweater) among Grygla friends of his hospital, circa 1920.

Another New Adventure

EARLIER, DAD AND Mother had moved from Ogema to Grygla for a new adventure. It was rumored that a twenty-mile railroad branch was to be extended from Goodrich, Minnesota. At that, time Grygla was typical of a small town situated in a farming area, inhabited mainly by homesteaders who could then have proximity to replenish supplies. The town lay on non-picturesque land with adjacent sparse groves of trees intersected by a small river a half-mile away. At times, the water level was high enough to allow us to swim naked in the pooled area under the bridge. In 1921, heavy rain overran the river, inundating the town in one foot of water. There was no crime, all homes were left unlocked. If, however, a door was locked, it could be opened with the ubiquitous skeleton key.

The houses were clapboard buildings adjacent to partly graveled dirt roads. When it rained large mud puddles would form, during which we kids would run splashing through them. In the early years, horses were the power source for wagons and sleds. Animal droppings dotted the roads, and during a dry, hot, windy day, dust mixed with horse manure would swirl down the street that crossed the small highway that ran east to west through the village.

Board sidewalks not only gave passage but also helped adults to scrape mud off their feet. Since the rough board was often the source of splinters in our bare feet, we learned to transgress gingerly over those hazards.

The town had no electricity, no water system or sewage plants. Oil lamps and lanterns were the main source of light while the mobile two-seater outhouses were used for human waste. One had the choice of either Sears Roebuck or Montgomery Ward catalog for wiping.

In this setting my father located his practice in an L shaped house, fitted for an office, living quarters, and space for three hospital beds, sometimes filled with birthing mothers. Since most all of the confinement cases at that time were carried out by midwives, initially he had very few cases. This abruptly changed after the following incident. He received a frantic call from a midwife to please rush out to the farm because she was fearful that the baby was dead. He told me when he applied a stethoscope to the patient's abdomen, he heard the faint fetal heart tones. He did what was necessary to correct the delivery complications and a healthy newborn resulted.

Prior to the birth, the husband, who was nervously pacing the floor, asked, "Doc, I don't know you; don't you think we should get further consultations?" Being non-diplomatic and obtrusive, dad answered, "Hell yes, go to the phone right now and call New York and get someone out right away." The midwife immediately left for greener pastures. The country doctor would travel to the patient's home and if necessary, stay until delivery, at times twenty-four hours or more. The ongoing rate for total care and delivery was twenty-five dollars.

In 1928 when my father returned to Thief River Falls, his obstetrical practice was far different from his same practice in Grygla. Being a no-nonsense person, one of his standards was not to induce labor unless definitely indicated. I often heard him repeat the saying, "The only time factor in a normal pregnancy is the uterus itself, not a scheduled timetable set-up by the mother, husband or doctor."

This proclamation put to test was related to me by his second wife, Alice, who was well acquainted with a minister's pregnant wife. The expectant delivery date had passed. After two or more weeks slipped by, the women members of the parish pleaded with her to discharge "Old Doc Adkins" and get the new young doctor who had recently opened his Thief River Falls practice. The minister's wife, however, retained her confidence in the "Old Doc." Confirming his patience, the mother, weeks after the expected date, had an uncomplicated delivery. The parish women were silenced.

Dad never mentioned that specific case to me, but he emphatically condemned the utilization of pentathol during the latter stage of labor. He said, "Yes it reduces maternal pain, but I am always fearful of the soporific effect on the fetus because the drug can cause depressed breathing and delayed resuscitation."

When pentathol, as an anesthetic, was innovated in the late thirties some doctors utilized it in order to minimize labor pains in spite of the possibility of having a fetus with immediate respiratory insufficiency, commonly called the "blue baby" syndrome.

(Later when I was interning, I too had an experience as a patient with overuse of pentathol. Dr. Arthur, an intern on the anesthesia service, administered pentathol to me for a urological study (retrograded ureteral pylogram). This followed an unpleasant attack of left renal colic. Following the anesthetic, I slept over twenty-four hours. Indeed, it caused some concern in the anesthesia department.)

Other Cases of a Country Doctor's Adaptability

MY FATHER, LIKE all country doctors, underwent many hardships and challenges. They were on their own: they had no available consultants. Only minimal laboratory facilities existed, and they had to travel by buggy or Model T Fords on frequently poor roads. House calls, rather than office calls prevailed. In the winter he utilized a horse drawn caboose, a small homemade shed-like structure, set on sled runners. For long trips in bitter cold weather, a small coal or wood burning stove was added. If the trips appeared hazardous, my father would leave notification of his route. Grabbing sleep whenever possible, he told me he went five days and four nights traveling in a caboose during the 1922 flu epidemic. Although the State Health Department offered flu vaccine, for which some doctors charged five dollars a shot, Dad utilized it without charge. He didn't believe its value had been substantiated. Instead, he said he had success in treating flu victims by having them sit by the stove. They were to stay warm wrapped in blankets and above all, to avoid going out into the cold until the symptoms had ceased. One woman left the sanctity of her home during her recovery period to attend a celebration. She had a relapse and died.

My father told me about an unusual surgical experience in which he acknowledged an element of self-pride. Dr. Stuarman asked him to come out to Erskin, Minnesota, to see a teenage boy who had a large bowel obstruction. The boy had eaten a voluminous amount of chokecherries, which had accumulated in an obstructing mass in the transverse colon. While smiling, my dad said he solved the challenge, not by opening the bowel, but simply by massaging the obstructing lump and then gently squeezing the berries into the lower colon and rectum, thus

26

allowing natural elimination. Evacuation of the berry meal through a bowel incision would have caused peritoneal contamination. Indeed, this case is unique, unlikely to be found in the surgical literature as one of the etiological factors of large bowel obstruction.

Other Endeavors

IN ADDITION TO medicine, Dad loved farming. He purchased two quarter sections of land about eight miles southwest of Grygla. Even though renters worked the land, Dad bought the tractors and machinery, plus supervising the planting assortment. On these trips, he would be dressed in soiled overalls. Many patients were upset when they saw him in this apparel.

It was on this farm where I spent long summers of hard work. While he had excellent medical judgment, his farming expertise was almost fantasy. Hoping to grow potatoes, he spent almost eight thousand dollars on a root house of his own design. It was a domed-shaped, concrete structure about six feet thick and covered with several feet of sod and soil. Although it was nice and cool, it never housed a potato.

How about raising chickens? He had a large chicken coop built with a south wall containing large glass panes. Ladder-like roosts were put up inside, and as I remember, I once saw about eight chickens pleasantly roosting there. It cost approximately eight hundred dollars.

How about raising sheep? A fifty-foot shed with a slanting roof was built; and instead of having a dirt floor, small poplar tree trunks were laid in side by side. I was given the task of packing hay between the poles in order to prevent injury to the sheep's feet and legs. It took me many hot mosquito and fly-infested days to complete the task. Of course, a sheep dip tank and ramp had to be made for the treatment of ticks. Very few sheep were ever purchased, thus escaping the sheep dip tank.

A small pig barn was also constructed. I once witnessed him performing a caesarean section on an overly obese full-term pig. This unusual event caused quite a stir in local community.

Since he admired Henry Ford, he purchased two Fordson tractors,

which constantly plagued us. During the very cold weather, the trans-
mission oil was removed, heated on the stove, and then replaced in
order to facilitate starting. During warm weather, the tractor would
spew steam, necessitating repeated radiator fills from multiple water
containers that we hauled into the field. Mechanical failures were frequent, thus requiring a sixteen-mile-round-trip by Ole Peterson, the
snuff-spitting mechanic. The early vintage Fordson, which had minimum pulling capacity, was useful primarily for mowing hay and pulling hayracks. The situations would have been cheaper and simplified
by the purchase of reputable makes.

A Lighter Side

EVEN THOUGH HE was usually quite somber, he sometimes displayed an enlightening spirit. When I came home to say goodbye to him before I was to enter the armed forces, something he said made me realize he had a subtle sense of humor. While we were making rounds at Mercy Hospital, he introduced me to an elderly patient as Dr. Douglas Adkins. She emphatically retorted, "There ain't to be a young whipper-snapper doctor taking care of me." He had a noticeable grin on his face as he reassured her that he would always be in charge. On that same visit in 1942 when I came home from my internship, he was smiling as he held open an envelope addressed to me, which contained an honorable discharge as a first lieutenant.

(All medical students were conscripted as first lieutenants after their graduation. I had received orders to report to Carlisle Barracks in Pennsylvania, on July 1, 1943. During my junior and senior years and my internship, I had repeated attacks of renal colic. The army ignored my signed waiver.)

A New Family Lifestyle

ASIDE FROM HIS devotion to medicine, I'm certain he did have moments of personal enjoyment. While he never took a day off, an exception was made when he went to Canada to marry his long-time nurse, Alice Solem. Dad was fifty-nine, Alice, thirty-eight. Two sons were born shortly; unlike the three sons of his first marriage who were strictly disciplined, he was not allowed to interfere with his new offspring. His wife had complete control of their supervision. He was almost a surrogate father. The brief episodes with his sons were precious to him. He loved butter, and he would feed them spoonful of this treat, to which his wife didn't object. She also allowed him to take the boys for car rides. He took great enjoyment holding them while they would alternate taking the steering wheel. At school, they were teased because of their parents' age discrepancies, perhaps leading to later adolescent problems.

Their undisciplined upbringing was exemplified by a table incident: once when I was home, their mother prepared an evening meal with apple pie for dessert. Pieces of pie were placed on the table adjacent to our plates. The boys, ages six and eight, each started to eat their pie immediately. Attempting to replace the pies, I said. "Dessert follows the meal." Alice immediately retorted, "If they want to eat their pie, they can do so." Dad sat silently. It was the first time in my life I saw a defeated look on his face, as opposed to the winning looks of the boys. (In his later life, he softened a bit toward his older children.)

Occasionally, during the three-month high school vacation farm work period, we would drive home, even though we were not especially welcomed by our stepmother. While she usually treated Jack and me very well, once when we were home she hastily grasped a fresh garden tomato from my hand. She said, "Those tomatoes are not for you." She seemed unusually upset about something so trivial. It so happened that Dad was standing nearby. He took me into the next room and gave me a dollar to purchase some tomatoes. He apologized by stating, "Sometimes women's actions stink during their pregnancies." (This reaction occurred prior to the birth of Peter, her second son.)

Discipline did come to the two miscreants, however, but not from my father. The mother was devastated when both boys were sent to reform school. She was so affected that for a time she lost her faith in God. My father took it in stride, envisioning the result of their juvenile behavior at the reform school, where they were forced to cut their shoulder-length hair. At this institution, a prodigious change took place. They matured when introduced to Oriental culture. Realizing that an environmental change was necessary, each took his college education money of fifteen thousand dollars and went to the Orient. Caylor, the eldest, studied in Japan, where he earned his black belt in Karate. Peter studied in China, later becoming an expert interpreter of the Chinese language.

As I conjure up the memory of my father, I see this stocky, determined man with is black bag always at his side, I wonder how many of my father's memories filled that black bag. It was his constant companion at any hour of the day or night, whether carried in summer in a buggy, or in winter, in a caboose over runners, or at times in Model T's, Model A's or V-8 Fords, and even a Packard. Through these multiple conveyances my father's resolve remained astute.

If it were horse drawn transportation, he could catch some much-needed sleep by simply dropping the reins. The horse always found the way home. These vehicles were transversed over unkempt slippery roads with deep ruts and mud puddles. In the winter, snow packed roads, often with large snowdrifts, had to be manipulated. One of my father's delights was to plow through un-seemingly, unconquerable snowdrifts. He had a reputation, like winning a blue ribbon, for the highest rate of rear-end car breakdowns.

Through all this travail, the leather companion was at his side. During those lonely hours on his way to the friendly homes, it helped him serve the young and the old. I envisioned him setting by the farm-house while the farmer would ask him to see an ill stock animal or proudly present a new bull or a new harness team. On the way back to the farmhouse to retrieve his bag, most likely he would have to stop and remove manure from his un-shined shoes, the doctor's bag always an icon of faded country doctors.

Bad Health and Revised Demeanor

DAD BECAME MORE amiable toward the end of his life. After suffering a stroke, he was admitted to Ft. Snelling Hospital in St. Paul, where he absolutely refused help from the physical therapy department. So he could listen to baseball games, I bought him a radio. On one occasion while I was sitting at his bedside, he displayed an element of hidden compassion when he gazed into my eyes and said, "Doug, you and I have always been great buddies, haven't we?" With tears in my eyes, I nodded, "Yes, Dad." I am certain he had deep compassion, but because of his stoic nature, he couldn't or wouldn't openly display it. I never saw him shed a tear, but my stepmother told me that when he was lying in the hospital bed at home, following his discharge from the VA, he would often cry while looking at the childhood oil paintings of my sister Arda and me.

My father, the country doctor, died at age eighty-two. His career ended while he was making rounds at Mercy Hospital in Thief River Falls, the same place where he had healed and cured so many patients in his early life. Following several strokes, he died three years later. To the end, his wife Alice grudgingly nursed him in their home. From the VA, she was able to obtain a hospital bed, similar to those he had stood beside so many times before, but to be used now for him only.

What is his legacy in the eyes of his children: Galen, Arda, Doug, Jack, Caylor, and Peter? At one time, his two youngest sons were ashamed of his age. Even though they were assured a college education due to his practice, I never heard any words of adulation for their father. In return, there was little emotion at his funeral.

Although I know Jack loved Dad, he never expressed his feeling for him. However, at the funeral, he nearly collapsed with grief. Arda, after she had received medicinal mental help, expressed her extreme dislike. Galen, who deeply loved his father and admired him as a doctor, yearned for the absent love. He once told me that Dad's Grygla patients either loved or hated him. I always thought he was beloved by all.

While he found it difficult to convey affection for his children, I know he had two deep loves; Minnie Hill, his first wife, and medicine.

Dad didn't attend funerals, including that of his handsome brother, who died of alcoholism, nor the one for his baby sister, Aunt Dora. When her college son died of pneumonia, he wasn't there to comfort her. Her grief was beyond description.

I am certain that part of his complete devotion to his practice was to assure his children of an education, and in that, he succeeded. The more important parts of a parent's duty, however, the showing of love, is where he failed.

Now, as my life's journey is short, how do I perceive my father? My feelings, too, are mixed. Indeed, I loved my father, but I was also fearful of him. His discipline inspired me to study hard to obtain my goals. However, I also believe he not only shortchanged his children, but also himself by not sharing close, joyful moments. Perhaps he wanted to show love, but just didn't know how. What we do know is that this complex person was constantly available and unselfishly administering to his patients—A COUNTRY DOCTOR WHOSE CLOSEST COMPANION WAS HIS DOCTOR'S BAG.

Dr. C.M. Adkin's winter conveyance, circa 1920.

Dr. Charles M. Adkins' 80th birthday party. Seated: Dr. Adkins, 2nd wife Alice Solum Adkins. Standing: sons Caylor, Jack, Doug, Galen, Curtiss.

Charles Marion Adkins and wife Minnie Hill on shooting range with friends in Thief River Falls, Minnesota.

Back row: Author (holding son Jones), Galen Adkins third from left, C.M. Adkins second from right; at left son Jack; middle row: Author's wife Eudora, stepmother Alice, Aunt Dora, the rest all Wisehart cousins.

Arda, Galen, author, father in Grygla, 1920 flood

BOOK II

Childhood Memories of Farm and

High School

Early Life amid the Seasons

WE MOVED FROM Grygla to Thief River Falls and then back to Grygla in my early childhood. My early memories of other people and times are myriad.

Winter

A winter incident nearly ended my life. While I was accompanying my sister, Arda and her childhood friends along the frozen Thief River, I noticed an area of open water (caused by hot water runoff from a nearby laundry). To satisfy my curiosity, I walked toward the water for a closer look. In doing so, I broke through thin ice; but by catching the ice's edge with my forearms, full submerging was prevented. Arda and her two friends pulled me out. Fortunately, we were only three blocks from home. Even so, I vividly remember the chilling short walk and the relief after my frightened mother dried me in warm blankets.

Although we were skeptical about the reality of Santa Claus, Christmas time was always exciting, especially because we looked forward to vacation days and winter fun. Playtime in the winter would consist of skiing, building caves in the snow banks, and skating on the frozen creek or on isolated ice ponds. Ice skates, which were clamped on our boots, would frequently fall off.

My second greatest possession as a child was a pair of shoe skates. On the first day of possession, I walked one fourth of a mile on the skates to a frozen gravel pit. Enthralled by the ease of gliding over the ice, I thought I was flying. Unfortunately, while entering the porch of our house I tripped and fell on a nail that was protruding from a board. The nail penetrated the knee joint. Dad sternly reprimanded my older brother for not removing nails from boards. My concerned father treated me with constant hot packs and rest. Fortunately, I had full recovery without infection, sepsis or tetanus.

One of the thrilling winter highlights consisted of sleigh riding on homemade sleds constructed out of two by four boards. A long rope was attached to the front of the sled, then threaded through the iron loop on the back runner of the farmer's sled. We then would be pulled out into the countryside. By pulling on the looped rope, we could maneuver the sled from side to side, especially when and if the farmer would gallop the horses. It was not unusual for us to walk four or five miles back to town. On bitter cold days our ears and noses would get partially frozen which needed treatment by snow application. Another winter pastime would be kicking or hitting frozen horse turds instead of tin cans.

Every Christmas the school children would engage in programs that would be held in the town hall. There was always a very tall pine Christmas tree with decorations and small candles held in place with a small snap on each candle holder. (It is a miracle that a fire never erupted.)

At one Christmas play an incident occurred which was both humorous and touching. The owner of the livery stable, who was poor, had two unattractive and very shy daughters. That evening the younger girl on stage with her school mates became frightened and inadvertently started to urinate. As the urine ran down her leg, forming a noticeable puddle at her feet, my kid brother Jack then walked onto the stage with his assignment. He was leading several of his classmates when he came to the puddle, then he stopped, looked, and walked around it. Each one that followed did likewise which caused some crude guffaws from the audience. Actually, it was a tragedy to a little girl during a gala event.

Spring

I remember each season with fondness, except for the boring work imposed by my father. Even though we had much fun with our winter activities, we anxiously looked forward to springtime not only for fun things but also realizing that the school year would soon be over. We would run over thin ice puddles that would crack and bend, hopefully without breaking. However, the ice did break on occasions, causing wet shoes and feet. It was difficult to wait for springtime, when bare feet would replace shoes and stockings. Of course, it was necessary to request permission. Surreptitiously, however, bare feet would prevail ahead of acquiescence.

One warm spring day while I was sitting on a board-wood sidewalk I noticed the mens' heavy shoes, wherein I said to myself, "I don't look forward to adulthood because then I will have to wear shoes." Only on rare occasions did I regret the bareness—after stubbing my toe, encountering slivers and inadvertently stepping into cow piles. The manure would slip up between my toes so then grass and sticks had to be used as cleaning aids. Another eagerly anticipated event was May Day, in which each child received fifteen cents worth of tokens usable for treats. We would ask each other "What are you going to buy? To what store are you going?"

While we had fun during the spring, we also had to work. In the garden near our house in Grygla it was my job, particularly, to keep it free of weeds by hoeing around the corn and removing bugs from the tomato plants. I had a hard time getting my brother Jack to work, the only way I could do so was by telling him stories. I would make up one story and then at the end of the story he would say, "Tell me another." This kept my mind in a swirl, but I was able to tell one story after another.

Dad who had given me a small hoe once took me out to a farm that was being run by the Burchet family. My job was to assist the Burchet boy in hoeing a small field of sweet corn. While we were working we kept a watch-out for nice stones. When we found an unusually pretty stone, we had an altercation about the owner. I became so upset that I put the hoe over my shoulder and walked bare-footed seven and one half miles back to our home in Grygla. I was eight years old at the time. My father apparently didn't like to see us idle, so he always seemed to have some work lined up. I remember once I had to strip the bark on a pile of fence posts stacked in our yard. The job was performed with a draw blade. Before I started, however, my father demonstrated the technique.

At about this age, I had the job of leading our Holstein cow down to Peterson's farm about a quarter mile east of town. In the summer it would be pastured at the farm, but in the wintertime we kept and fed it in the barn. Often I had to milk this cow. It was a task that I didn't enjoy because of the switching of the cow's tail and the difficulty of getting all of the milk to go into the pail instead of on my knees. The only enjoyable part of milking was when I squirted milk into the open mouths of one of our many barn cats. One year the cats feasted on fourteen dead mice that we had killed while haying.

Summer

The summers seemed to quickly end. Even though I had chores, there were many enjoyable times. Dad always gave us instructions: wood had to be split and piled in the porch, the garden must be hoed, and the barn cleaned (we had one cow). We helped with the haying of an adjacent twenty-acre alfalfa field, following which we went to the pool hall and were treated with ice-cream sundaes. Of all the summer jobs, hay times were the most pleasant and "weed pulling" the most despised. The farm was seven miles southwest of Grygla. Before I was able to drive, I rode with brother Galen to my main job of "weed pulling."

Adults paid little attention to the children during those days, so during the summer the boys occupied themselves in various ways. Father rarely played with us; however, in his youth he liked baseball. Consequently, he did play catch with us, if infrequently.

We all had homemade slingshots, fashioned from a Y-shaped branch to which were tied rubber bands cut from a discarded inner tube. Connected to the rubber was a small leather pouch that held a small selected stone. After many hours of practice, we became quite expert at hitting bottles and tin cans. I once cried when I inadvertently shot and killed a robin. However, for some reason sparrows were fair game. In another sad moment, I killed a swift flying swallow that actually flew into the pellet.

We also flew homemade kites. Since garden snakes were abundant, we once tied a small snake onto the tail of the kite and lofted it into the air. We then released the snake with its partially damaged tail. We also did other devious pranks; such, as catching any stray dog that had escaped the jaws of the local bully dog name Tigue. Tin cans were then tied to the tail of the unfortunate stray which would run out of town, never to return. Another mischievous act was to catch frogs, gleefully putting them into several cars that were parked outside the town hall.

We played games such as Anti-I-over, Follow the Leader, and Run Sheep Run. Because we ran barefooted during the summer, the soles of our feet hardened, enabling us to run over graveled dirt roads. The small town had wooden sidewalks from which occasionally we got slivers in our feet. Also while running we could stub our big toe.

Our clothing consisted of one pair of overalls which we could easily shed while running towards the swimming hole. The last one in was called an "old maid." Also we would play King of the Hill on the straw stacks which in winter were used as ski hills.

Having no allowance, we had to find ways of obtaining pocket money. At that time there was a bounty on gopher tails and crows' feet: a gopher tail would bring us five cents and a pair of crows' feet fifteen cents. In order to catch a gopher, we would either set a trap near its hole, or if water were available, we would pour it down the hole. When the gopher would come up for air, execution was accomplished with a yielded stick.

Another method of picking up some spare change was by selling copper tubing, discarded radiators, aluminum and a certain type of rubber car tires. These were sold to a Jewish peddler that came to Grygla once or twice each summer. Our elders advised us to negotiate with him, but we rarely prevailed.

At one time, with difficulty, I did make a few dollars by passing out the Sunday edition of the *Minneapolis Tribune*. I didn't keep very accurate account of the money; consequently, a representative of the paper cam to Grygla and confronted me. My Dad got it all straightened out. I had a small safe in which I put my money, and for security I buried in under our front proch.

We had a lot of fun rolling a tire or utilizing a homemade wheel and pusher. The four-foot pusher was a lath to the end of which we nailed a twelve-inch lath. We became very adept at pushing a metal wheel up and down small mounds and curves. Also, we made our own stilts and became quite adept at walking on upgraded areas and even going up small steps. We had a difficult time attaching the stirrup to the walking pole, however.

We looked forward to "Ladies Aid Day" in which the women would hold a church social food sale. The kids would indulge in potato salad, triple layered chocolate cake, and lefse, the popular Norwegian food. Often we would slip some lefse into our pockets before leaving the church.

One summer when my friend Clayton and I were nine, we received a mighty sum of five dollars each for splitting a huge pile of wood and stacking it in a wood shed. We worked on and off for two and one half months. Also we each picked up five dollars when we herded about fifty cattle to Goodridge, which was about fifteen miles south of Grygla. During the sojourn, we noticed frequent breeding episodes after which I asked my father, "What was all that fluid that kept running out of their rear ends?" I don't remember what his response was. At that age we obviously were aware that storks didn't bring babies into the world, but we were not knowledgeable about the physiology of fertilization.

During prohibition, home brewing was very common. Eudora and her sister Rhoda used to help their father by washing and capping bottles. He had the reputation of being the best brew master in the vicinity. During the summer on an off day of farm work, Clayton and I drank enough green beer that was fermenting in a large crock on his grandfather's porch to make us gloriously inebriated. I showed off to Clayton by running bare legged through a patch of thistles. I also remember telling him how much I hated the job of pulling weeds on the farm. (I also pushed away little islands of mold so we could dip with our cups.) I became extremely sick with nausea, projectile vomiting, topped off with a pounding headache. I told my brother Galen but fortunately my father didn't find out.

Fall

We especially looked forward to fall thrashing time when we were allowed to drive a team of horses between the rows of grain shocks while the farmer pitched the grain onto the wagon. All of us barefooted, we frequently encountered thistles that infiltered the grain bundles. We also enjoyed the abundant food prepared by the farmers' wives. At midmorning and mid-afternoon, massive lunches were served. We would devour the food and at times were even allowed to have a few sips of aromatic coffee. Also, during the fall we picked choke cherries, thus choking our pockets with cake and smashed choke cherries. Other pockets would be filled with selected stones used for the slingshots.

On Halloween nights, adults would party, but it was the custom for the kids to soap store windows and the teenagers to tip over "back houses." To get even, an owner once moved the house a few feet forward, causing the assailants to "fall in."

As in all seasons every Saturday was bath day. The ritual took place in a washtub placed in the center of the kitchen. Warm water was removed from the stove's reservoir or from the stove kettles. In the summer it didn't seem necessary to take a bath because we swam in the river, of course, with no soap. Once in a while I did have the luxury of taking a bath in the hospital bathtub. Another distressing duty took place prior to bed time. Jack and I would try to escape the ritual of "wash your feet." I never remember being told to wash our hands after toilet use or before meals.

Author, brother Jack and pet dog named Jack.

Author holding two adopted lambs

Haying time on farm. From left: father, unidentified worker, Galen on tractor, hired man Lester, author on Dodge truck.

Birthday party for author on steps of Grygla Hospital. Sister Arda holding Doug.

Mother's Legacy

WHEN IT BECAME evident that there was to be no railroad branch and because of that, the small community had no prospects of growth, Dad and Mother then moved back to Thief River Falls for greater opportunity. Jack and I were born in Grygla. At the time of the move, we were one and three years of age. (Dad had delivered both of us.)

It was in Thief River when mother became very ill. I poignantly remember her crying out with pain when Jack crawled over her abdomen, at which time I hastily pulled him off. Her death was a tragic event that affected the rest of the family during their entire lives. Initially, for many months, I cried myself to sleep and forevermore have grieved for her. For many years we kept her memory alive by putting a dozen roses on her grave on each of our birthdays.

In Thief River Falls, we had moved into a three-story, seven-bedroom, locally made red brick house constructed in 1898. It had a graceful stairway with a long banister railing well adapted for sliding. Beautiful stained glass adorned all the windows and doors. Noisy water radiators heated the upstairs while most of the heat from downstairs came through a large grate above the coal-burning furnace. We would often warm up by standing on the grate.

It was in this house where mother, at age thirty, tragically passed away from some type of abdominal aliment. While I don't remember many things about her, the ones that remain are deeply engrained. A sad day was at my mother's funeral, held in the living room of our house. Dad held me in his arms as I kissed my mother's cheek. Strangely, I refused him when he asked me if I wanted to kiss her again.

I remember several incidents in regard to my mother. One time she and I took a train to Kansas City in order to visit her family. There, at age three, I remember seeing a large staircase and nearby, a picture of

50

her Navy brother in uniform. I am bewildered that I don't remember more of the journey except that she had on a large hat.

Another distinct memory involved eating a peach. I was puzzled by the pit until my mother informed me that if I planted it, a large tree would grow. I immediately went outside and planted it in the ground with visions of some day having peaches. Years later when I returned, there was no peach tree. In spring when the robins invaded our yard, a family visitor told me I could catch a robin by simply putting salt on his tail. Soon several close attempts discouraged me.

Two other disappointments occurred during the relationship with my mother. One incident involved my mother and a bachelor friend of my father. They were sitting at the table drinking tea when I heard him relate his cabin experiences at the northwest angle at the Lake of the Woods. I was fascinated by his dog's ability to carry wood sticks in his mouth and then deposit them in the wood box. He accepted my request to go back with him, but this was quickly repulsed with laughter after I came downstairs with a pillowcase filled with a few meager belongings.

One summer day after playing outside, I asked the maid where my mother was, only to be informed that she had accompanied my father to Fourtown. When I learned that Fourtown was only one town rather than four towns together, I was very disappointed. Fourtown was named because it consisted of a creamery and a small store situated at the corner of four land sections.

On the other hand, memories of my father at this period of my life are more varied. One of the joyous times was the day Dad bought me a tricycle, the first of my two prized childhood possessions. I also remember when he took me out to the shotgun practice range. The only thing that I was interested in was picking up the empty shell cases. Years later after I had the tricycle, I repeatedly pleaded for a bicycle, but was always denied.

Author with mother in Kansas City shortly before her death in 1920.

Music

WHILE MUSIC WAS not important in our lives, I am very certain we would have had a greater appreciation if mother had lived. As a legacy, she left six large records with the title of each album written in dainty handwriting inside the cover. Arias of famous opera singers such as Enrico Caruso, Richard Tucker and Lawrence Melchoir were included. One of the old records was Jenny Lind, singing "Whispering Hope" (Dad's favorite song). We played many of the records on the old cabinet upright Victrola, usually using only wooden needles (Dad's absolute orders). Occasionally we did use steel needles, which caused scratching trauma to many records. Some of the records were very heavy and thick.

Dad seldom listened to the music, but when he did, he liked to listen to the famous Scottish singer and entertainer Harry Lauder, who sang, "It's nice to get up in the morning, but it's nicer to stay in your bed." Although sister Arda progressed well on the piano, I never recall Dad's asking her to play or any effort to reinforce her natural talent. While in high school, Jack and I took piano lessons, but to no avail. Dad owned a guitar that had a good tone, but rarely did he strum it. It was borrowed by Wisehart cousins, but never returned. Our father persistently refused to buy us a radio with no explanation as to why.

Back to Grygla

AFTER MOTHER'S DEATH, in order to sleep, Dad started to drink. He was fearful of the consequences. Despite making fifteen thousand dollars a year and having the promise of a new hospital, Dad felt that a change of venue was necessary. One year later, we moved back to Grygla, where we lived in a one-story "L" shaped house that Dad had previously used as his office and living quarters when he first moved there from Ogema.

At that time, Dad had a small room for his office, and adjacent to that there was a larger portion that had sufficient room for three patients' beds. A kitchen, pantry, living room, and two bedrooms completed the floor plan. Heating was by a large wood burning potbellied stove. We were able to view the flames through the glass on the stove door. The large upright wood burning kitchen stove had an adjacent reservoir that supplied hot water. Nearby stood the large slop pail. There were no sinks and consequently dish and hand washing plus table scraps were disposed into the pail. When it was brimming full, it had to be carried out and dumped next to the outhouse, about forty feet away. In the winter, a motley crown of ice was formed.

We entered the kitchen through the attached porch, which was used for wood storage, boots and overshoes. Dishes, pots and pans were kept in a large pantry. The room next to the small office, where Dad had kept patients was called the "back room." While we all slept well in the back room, I remember one night when I had a frightening nightmare. I was awakened by a terrible dream where I saw waves of German soldiers coming to town. I quickly got out of bed, walked past the garden, and crawled under a barbed wire fence with the thought of hiding under the bridge. When I crawled under the barbed wire the grass, which was covered with dew, tickled my belly. Instead of running down to the river to a hiding place, I went back inside and woke up my father. I told him to quickly get out of bed and save us from the Germans. He told me that it wasn't happening, and with that assurance I crawled under the covers and finally fell asleep.

My sister had her own bedroom. Because there was no stove in our bedroom, during the cold winter nights when the temperature fell below zero, we would dash into the bed and jump under the heavy-laden covers. Prior to this, our fully- covered leg and soiled- foot pajamas were put on while we stood by the big potbellied stove that was in the living room. Before we were dressed with pajamas, Dad's "rub on" had to be applied to our chests (Everyone in the community had Doc's rub on, consisting of a mixture of one-third oil of wintergreen and two-thirds olive oil). We preferred Dad's application because of his soft hands rather than the housekeeper's rough scratchy ones. He rubbed us infrequently, however, because he was usually at the hospital. On rare occasions when he was home before our early bedtime, he would hold and rock us in the large red leather rocking chair by the stove.

In the wintertime, instead of utilizing the backhouse, at night we used a porcelain pail whose contents would become completely frozen during the cold nights. During the fall, one of our jobs was to nail tarpaper along the lower three feet of the house, which we then had to "bank up" with manure from the barn. This was the only house insulation. Of course, in the spring it all had to be carried away.

People and Places

Earlier, when Dad and Mother had moved from Ogema to Grygla, the population at that time was about one hundred fifty people. There were two general stores, one cooperative and one private, two banks, a small hotel, a small post office, a tiny telephone office, an oil station and garage, creamery, barbershop, blacksmith shop, livery stable and a so-called drug store that sold proprietary medicine.

As in all communities, extreme characters imprint my childhood memories. There was the bachelor Soley, who had a small shoe repair shop with a classical smell of leather and stain. He was, at least at one time, profoundly religious. During a below zero winter night he climbed on the roof of his small house and sat facing east while patiently waiting for Christ's return. He was religiously blessed with only frozen fingers and toes that necessitated amputation, leaving only a few stumps. Since Soley's office was just across the street from our L-shaped one-story home, I would go to his shop to observe this now digit-less man maneuver needles and small instruments with the use of his mouth and a few finger stumps. In spite of his impairment, his repairs were quite artistic. I admired his expertise.

On the other end of town, there was another small building occupied by Moses, an Asian with classical olive skin and dark eyes. He was an excellent photographer who utilized the old head and cloak type camera. In order to subsidize his meager income, he sold moonshine (white lightning). In the back room of his shop, he constructed a small still to make alcohol. After entering his house, a person was immediately cognizant of the sweet smell of fermenting mash.

In order to pick up a few pennies for candy, my friend Clayton Moran and I would sell Moses empty bottles. Even though we obviously knew what they were for, we would ask, "Moses, what are they for?" "Making ketchup," he replied. Although Moses was a very lonely man, ostracized by the community, he saved enough white lightning money to purchase a second-hand Model T. His ownership was short lived, however. While maneuvering down an alley, he ran into the side of the post office. Later, while endeavoring to assist the post office mistress who was walking home, he bumped her. Her heavy coat saved her life, but for Moses it was the *coupe de grace*.

The cornerstone of Grygla was Harold Bush's barbershop where local news and gossip would be spread, pipe smoked, tobacco chewed, and spittoons aimed at. There was a ritual for the shaving process. The customer would be laid back in the one-barber chair, and a hot steaming towel would then be applied to the face. While the stubble was being marinated, in order to soften the whiskers, Bush would reach for one of the leather straps hanging nearby. He would grab it like a horse's tail and rhythmically and deftly slap, slap the razor, first on the rougher side, then the more glistening one, in order to fine tune the edge. He would then moisten his thumb, check the edge and remove the towels.

The shaving process would then be initiated. First, while raising a nostril, he would shave the upper lip. The chin was pulled up from the neck and the cheeks stretched for their service. He gently held the black-handled razor with his little finger extended as though he were drinking out of a demitasse cup. After the shaving was completed, he would apply an astringent of either Bay Rum or Lucky Tiger, whose fragrance I especially liked. Occasionally we would pick up a nickel or a pool chip when we were asked to give up our place in line. Bush reinforced us with common comments such as, "Good luck will come to you if you find an old horseshoe or a four leaf clover." At that time, he used hand clippers for haircuts. He very rarely took a vacation and barbered into his late eighties.

Next to the barbershop was a pool hall with a large counter where you could purchase glasses of Green River, Coca Cola or an ice cream cone. At the end of the counter was a cigar and tobacco cabinet, on top of which were a flickering gas lighter and cigar tip cutter. A distant cousin of mine became inquisitive and learned the hard way when he put a finger into the cigar cutter. Of course, the ubiquitous spittoons were placed in spitting range, but well away from several tables where people could enjoy ice cream sundaes.

The back room contained a pool table and several card tables where customers played pinochle. Since gambling was illegal and legal tender was not used, pool chips, good only at the pool hall, were passed out. It was taboo for women and children to enter that sanctuary, but from the area where I was allowed, I can still remember the loud banging and gleeful laughing as the winning card was slapped on the table.

Another nostalgia was the cooperative, commonly called the "co-op store." The hardware department was in the rear, the dry goods department in the front, and the meat and groceries in between. Side shelves contained various types of clothing, such as overalls and shirts. Wooden boxes of overshoes and boots lined the aisles. We kids would often sit in them and dangle our bare feet over the side just to observe the customers.

A very friendly man by the name of Mickey Sheldrew managed the store, but the hardware department was run by a very loveable man named John Bjornstad. Everybody liked John Bjornstad, especially the children, and he, them. When he came to the store on Sundays, and if we could catch him, he would give us a really big bag of candy for five cents. Although he was advised not to by the store management, he continued to give us a big order for a nickel. While he liked to imbibe, he was never obnoxious or unreasonable. His department was another gathering place for adult jabbering. During an open air picnic where the food was spread out on the ground, he once told my dad he would like to see a group of young children just turn loose on the spread.

I recall a barrel of lutefisk in which long slabs where pulled out of the brine, weighed, and sold during the festive holidays. Barrels of penny-size nails sat side by side on the linseed stained floor, while on the walls, hung farm tools such as scythes, pitchforks, shovels and leather harness straps. A potbellied stove stood in the center of the room, where customers would frequently open the door and utilize the stove as a spittoon. Lumber was stored in a shed located behind the hardware store. I liked the smell of fresh lumber. All store supplies were hauled forty miles from Thief River Falls. Johnny Manney was the trucker, and everyone was amazed at his agility, strength, and ability to maneuver large and heavy objects in spite of his five-foot seven-inch stature.

John Viking's blacksmith shop, on the one main street, was the epitome of the poem "Under the spreading chestnut tree, the village smithy stands." I was fascinated by the shop's contents and activities. In a large glowing coal pit, John would insert irons that would be sculptured with his heavy iron hammer onto the adjacent large anvil. Sparks would fly as he hammered the white iron into the different sculptured stages. We had to be extremely careful not to get hit on our bare legs by flying sparks. Following the initial blow, the hammer would often produce a staccato on the anvil. This was followed by repeated strikes until there was satisfaction with the finished product. Frequent insertions into the hot red coals were needed. The bed of coals was kept hot by an adjacent fan motorized by a hand turned blower, which we were often allowed to turn. A barrel of water was nearby for inserting hot finished products, thus producing bubbling and hissing steam. Multiple long tongs were used to handle hot parts.

A variety of objects to be fixed were also scattered about inside and outside. Unsharpened plow shares waiting their turn to be hammered into a proper soil cutting edge littered the well-packed floor. He shod the big horses and, after deftly fashioning the proper fit, would lift the leg and nail on the shoe. Needless to say, he was always busy.

This mustachioed, quiet and soft-spoken man was one of the few men in town who didn't chew tobacco. He had a very intelligent daughter and a not-so-bright son named Tilford. The latter once tied the tails of two cats together and hung them over a clothesline. He was quiet and shy and would frequently step off the sidewalk to allow us to pass. Exceptionally slow in school, he frequently would blow his nose with a resounding force into a large red or blue handkerchief.

Although I was infrequently in the Viking's house, I once reprimanded Tilford after he had finished kicking his mother. I said "Tilfey, don't do that. I don't have a mother." During the extreme cold winter days, he was so enveloped in clothes that when he got to school he could barely maneuver his arms or breathe or see over his muffled face. In later years, his sister Ann became a librarian, and I heard that Tilfey had a successful business life in Chicago.

Near the blacksmith shop was a general store owned by the Browns, a very religious couple who gained a reputation of various methods of cheating. Unfortunately, they had twins who were subject to epileptic seizures, especially initiated by episodes of stress such as sudden fright (we obnoxiously called them the Brown turds). All of us kids were requested to refrain from such deviling. However, this wasn't followed one-hundred percent. Occasionally, we would jump out from the side of the building to frighten them, which caused frothing of the mouth and epileptic arm, leg and head seizures.

Another pertinent building, the town hall, was kitty-corner from the creamery. It held dances, plays, Christmas programs, community meetings, and silent movies—primarily westerns with Tom Mix and Ken Maynard. I had the job of posting upcoming films. We played cowboy games in which we harangued as to who would be Tom Mix or Ken Maynard. A sequel, "Last of the Mohicans," was featured; as I remember, it portrayed the Indians as marauding savages. I clearly recall one episode when during an attack on a white settlement, an Indian smashed an infant's head against a tree. The only place to sit was in rows of wooden benches, the little kids, age six to seven in the front row and the big kids, ages up to fourteen, in back. The older boys tormented us from behind by throwing paper balls or making jokes about us.

The projectionist, who brought the flicks from Thief River Falls, forty miles away, operated from a rear balcony called "Nigger Heaven" (as kids we knew nothing of that connotation). During an occasional dance, parents would house their children in these balcony rows until the wee hours of the morning. The movies were frequently interrupted by film breakage, during which the only sounds heard were the slapping of the broken film and utterances such as, "Oh, no. Not again." After watching the movie "Frankenstein," I had a nightmare. I couldn't sleep because of the street scene in which Frankenstein was trudging with a small girl in his arms (since then I can never watch a horror movie).

The telephone office was in a small building with a plug-in switchboard. The operators lived in the same edifice. Instead of numbers, each phone would have rings, which consisted of long, and short. In order to call someone, you would turn the small telephone handle according to their proper number of rings. There was hardly a need for a newspaper because people would "rubber" in. A private conversation wasn't possible.

There was, however, a newspaper called "The Grygla Eagle," made by a printing press. Every word had to be constructed with small lead strips, each containing a letter or symbol. My good friend, Clayton

Moran, became very adept at constructing words while assisting his grandfather, the owner of the paper.

Two relatively short-lived banks served the community. The demise of one bank was hastened by the manager's embezzlements. He was literally run out of town, in spite of being the son of a well-respected farmer.

Even though there was a scarcity of cars and tractors, Grygla did have a garage with a tall hand gasoline pump. Mr. Fladland, the long-mustachioed proprietor, who always sat in front of the garage, was a permanent fixture. Although he was a quiet man, I always felt uneasy in his presence. Even more disconcerting was Ole Petersen, the mechanic. Always in our bare feet, we had to skip away from him because he seemed to take delight in spitting tobacco juice on our legs and feet.

A less active structure was Sordahl's small feed mill. The family lived in a two-story house that had a dirt floor. The mother, a buxom woman who was always barefoot, nursed the children up to four years of age. Even though they weren't noted for cleanliness, she was recognized for her bread and bun making. The family was also noted for having hair lice. (My dad treated the problem with kerosene shampoos.) Dad would often advice us to study and work so that we wouldn't grow up to be like the Sordahls. I knew that one of the girls my age who had head lice became a very successful Mary Kay beauty aid salesperson, traveling around towns in her pink Cadillac.

Author on current Grygla street

The Adkins' home, Thief River Falls, Minnesota.

Old swimming hole

Soley's Shoe Shop

Present-day Grygla

Schools and Religion

SUMMER VISITORS CHANGED the face of the town. Being religious, the Fladland family would host tent meetings for the "Holy Rollers." We kids would stick our heads under the tent flaps and observe the wild antics of yelling and rolling in the aisles. Also, we would follow the procession to the river wherein, accompanied by mournful prayers, baptism would take place by total submersion. We children were astonished by the crazy behavior of grown men and women. It was like going to a circus.

The Pentecostals, however, were not the only amusement in town. Almost every summer another tent show of family itinerant thespians would arrive. They would stay for several days, putting on a nightly play. Before and after the show, bottles of proprietary medicine were offered for sale by use of the "pitch." Liquid panacea for most common ailments would be offered. Also, gypsy wagons with their bright and motley dressed occupants, would occasionally "hit" the town. They would wander around, attempting to tell fortunes and sell trinkets. Friendly and gregarious, they were in no way scary, in spite of the rumors that they "stole" children and were "lightfingered" with people's property. Since the townspeople regarded them as handsome and entertaining visitors, they were never chased out of town.

All of the townspeople came out to see the next summer visitor who arrived by air in a WW I bi-plane. The barnstorming pilot landed his plane in Peterson's alfalfa field just east of town. Very few people paid the fee for the air view of the countryside.

We went to school in a two-room schoolhouse that had a belfry and a shed at each end for coats and overshoes. We would vie for the privilege of ringing the bell. The rooms were heated with big potbellied wood stoves. Outside and away were the two "outhouses," each with two holes that were rarely deep enough to hold the odiferous contents. Each toilet featured the familiar catalogs for cleansing purposes. I distinctly recall there was nothing for hand washing. To get permission for relief, one hand was held up for urination and both hands for defecation.

Each morning in the big room, we would sing. Our teacher would play the piano to a song that we were asked to choose. My brother Jack, two years younger, always jumped up and yelled, "Yankee Doodle."

The little room contained grades from one through five, after which the students graduated to the big room. Each student had a small desk onto which was attached a chair. The desk contained an ink well and a tray for pencils, the desktop invariably stained with ink and brutalized with knife carvings.

Although usually well-disciplined, we did some devilment by wrapping paper around a .22 caliber bullet and tossing it into the stove, thus producing a popping noise. We would fold up paper in order to make a small airplane for arching across the room. We also made a small, potential dangerous dart. Utilizing the so-called farmer's "match," we inserted a sewing needle into one end, broke off the phosphorous end, split it and inserted a paper fin. The missile could be sailed across the room with some accuracy. Fortunately, there were never any casualties.

I looked forward to the freedom of school vacation, but not to Sunday school. Religion played only a minor role in our family. While Dad never went to church, we had to go year-round to Sunday school, which I thoroughly disliked.

We were assigned poems to memorize, which I perceived to be stupid and meaningless. One wintry day, I was almost gleeful when I was unable to attend Sunday school class. Later, Mrs. Brown, our Sunday school teacher, asked why I missed last week's class. I explained that while I was dumping the kitchen slop pail onto the icy mound near the outside toilet, I slipped and the slop soaked my only pair of pants. I had no replacement.

We were also constantly reminded to say our bedtime prayer which began: "Now I lay me down to sleep, if I should die before I wake, I pray the Lord my soul to take." If Dad went to bed at our time, he would repeat; "Be sure to say your prayers" or "Did you say your prayers?" I don't recall him every saying a prayer. It bewildered me.

Perhaps these early negative experiences with religion caused me to react in a cynical way much later in my life. Once when I was a patient myself, a religious representative of some denomination came into my room to console me. She asked, "What is your religious affiliation?" I replied, "I belong to the Round Church." She asked, "What church is that? I've never heard of it before." I said, "That's the church where the devil can't corner you." With a disdainful look on her face, she quickly left the room.

Grade School Romance

I FIRST MET EUDORA Hawkins when I was four years-old. Her family had moved to Grygla from a nearby farm. It was on this farm that my dad had delivered Eudora. He was the first one to ever see her. After mother died, and after we moved back to Grygla, Eudora and I became very fond of one another, playing together, going on sleigh rides and having marshmallow roasts.

Since Rhoda, Eudora's sister, was two years older, she entered kindergarten before Eudora, who repeatedly pleaded to attend as well. The teacher accepted her as a passive measure. Eudora immediately succeeded and retained that desire for learning for the rest of her life. Later we were in the school's "big room" together.

In a premeditation of our love, an implausible occurrence took place. It was the custom to have Valentine exchanges between the thirty pupils. The boys would put their names in one box, the girls in another. Then each pupil would reach in and draw a name for a Valentine exchange. I drew Eudora's name and she drew mine. I remember buying her a very lacy Valentine. Some time later, we also shared a food basket I purchased at the community hall basket social. I immediately bid two dollars on the one, which I knew to be hers. Dad questioned my judgment. I had the only bid.

Our lives soon intertwined again. Even though the Hawkins family moved to Thief River Falls in 1926, we found a way to meet. When Eudora visited her cousin who lived in Grygla, we would get together. When Dad remarried in 1931, we moved back to Thief River Falls, where Eudora and I again went to school together, continuing our romance in high school. She graduated from high school one year ahead of me because I only received one year's credit for the two-year six-month course at Crookston.

Childhood and Sex

IN CHILDHOOD, EVEN though hormonal blood level of estrogen and testosterone is infinitesimal, there is an inherent curiosity for the other gender. One summer day my friend Clayton and I were playing in an empty icehouse with two girls our own age of seven or eight. We said, "We'll show you ours if you'll show us yours." I don't know what I had expected, but I remember seeing just some bare skin.

At about the same age I experienced something more perplexing. I had accompanied my father on some type of journey to a distant farm; and for some reason, there was an overnight stay. Apparently, the bedrooms were sparse, so I was bedded with a pubescent girl. During the night, I was awakened by her twiddling my tiny penis with her finger. In later life, I surmised that being unable to sleep, instead of counting sheep, she was counting the twiddles.

Although there had been childhood curiosity, my metamorphosis, a teen-age sexual experience, started at age thirteen with my first romantic kiss. Eudora, my love object, was in Grygla visiting her cousin Helen Miller and her family, who lived in an apartment on the top of an old bank. Eudora and I were sitting on the enclosed steps leading to the apartment. It was there where I kissed her. I was so enthralled that I told my friend Clayton, and with his hand over his heart, he promised to keep it a secret. About the same time as the kissing episode (I was now an expert) I had another experience that perplexed me. While I was necking with a nearby farm girl, she took my hand and directed it under her dress to a certain place. "Right there," she said. Obviously, it was her clitoris, but at that age, to me an unknown entity.

Sexual learning has stages. About five years later, I was puzzled again. I had borrowed by brother's car to drive a girl home from a dance at the old community hall. While we were engaged in a prolonged goodnight-kissing episode, she began to tremble and shake. It was a warm evening, so I knew it wasn't a cold weather response. After some inquiry, I was told her action was a spontaneous passion response. Later, I informed my dad that I had met this beautiful farm girl. He said, "Stay away from that family because they are full of tuberculosis." I never saw her again

In my teen-age years, I came close to the "real thing." One warm spring evening during my senior high school year, I had a spontaneous erotic episode—which could have been a disaster. My friend Gibby Granum and I went to a country dance where we met two female classmates. During the dance break, we went into the car for a necking party. My partner and I took the back seat, Gibby and his date, the front. Our passionate effervescence led to a mutual point of pending intercourse; however, I am forever grateful for the intervention of Mother Nature's serendipity. Apparently, the heat of our passion attracted an invasive army of mosquitoes that would have ravaged our bare skin. We quickly cooled off and went back to dance. My initiation had to come later.

College (High School)

AFTER GRADE SCHOOL, at age thirteen, I was sent to Crookston Agricultural College. I received no explanation. Did he do so because of transportation problems to the nearest high school in Goodrich fifteen miles away where Arda went or was it a subtle method of not having to cope with me? Certainly, it wasn't for a higher education as preparation for my pre-determined medical career.

My father drove me to Crookston, where we had lunch prior to matriculation. I remember putting a nickel in the music box and openly cried as it played "Home Sweet Home." When I saw the large campus inhabited by the farm kids, I was awakened into reality. It was a shocking change from the Grygla two-room schoolhouse. I was introduced to farm culture such as judging pigs and heifers, plus culling chickens. Since I was unaware of most of the agricultural disciplines, I had to study especially hard for those subjects. I was totally at a loss in the judging pits. Pigs and heifers all looked alike to me. I made my grade selection purely by chance, not unlike tossing a coin or saying "eenie, meenie, minie, moe." The subjects I liked best were mechanical drawing, shorthand and typing, especially typing because the teacher was a beautiful black haired Irish girl named Fay Highbanks. Aside from judging, my grades were satisfactory.

While I was lonesome, school presented a challenge. My loneliness was modified by my first view of an indoor swimming pool and assignment to a seat beside the coach at the basketball court. For the latter, I was given a small emergency kit containing band-aids, swabs and mercurochrome—my first medical position. Another of my jobs was raising the flag each morning. One time I was embarrassed when informed that the flag was upside down. I also sat by the coach at football games, which seemed to me to be a brutal sport. During one game after being

71

rendered semi-unconscious, a player lay on the ground vomiting greenish bile gastric content. Being only thirteen and weighing only one hundred and ten pounds, I was frightened by the rough sport. Even so, during a student participation sports outing, I received first place in diving competition; however, I cried after I lost a three-minute, three round boxing match. I wasn't a worthy opponent for the farm boy.

Since dormitory nights were very cold, I would get up early and study through the morning. I was enclosed in an overcoat along with a stocking cap and overshoes. The early rising afforded me ready access to the commonly overcrowded bathroom and toilet facilities. On parents' day, our room had to pass inspection. I was devastated, as the only one whose parents didn't show up.

Most of my dormitory experiences had little to do with classroom education. It was popular practice for one of the stronger boys to wrap his arms around the lower chest of another boy from behind and squeeze hard while holding him off the floor, (similar to the Heimlich procedure). The individual would then temporarily pass out. When it came my turn, in order to frighten them, I pretended to be still knocked out. One boy, who thought I was faking, held a very foul smelling stocking in front of my nose. It was stifling, but I remained prone. Unconvinced, they left me on the floor and went off to a meal. I skipped my meal and when they returned I was up and about. My reaction must have had an affect, because I believe they quit doing it. I never confessed my ploy.

While living in the dormitory I revealed my thirteen-year-old naiveté when I was introduced to masturbation. A group of upper classmen made a student demonstrate his unusually large penis. Just before ejaculation, he started to say, "It's coming." Observing this event, I innocently asked, "How does he know?" The older boys in unison laughed and said, "He knows!"

Another more personal experience involved my entrepreneurship. I bought boxes of candy, Babe Ruth, Snickers, Hershey, and profited by selling them in the dormitory. My cash transactions were kept in a bureau drawer. My roommate, Norman Theiling (a Grygla area farm boy with persistent extremely nauseating stinky feet and stockings) caught another farm boy attempting to steal my cash. Angry, I reported him to the main office, where an interrogation followed. He was expelled.

An unexplained experience occurred when a curly haired older student invited me to accompany him to a downtown Crookston movie. While seated in the theatre, he put his left arm around my shoulder, periodically fidgeting with my left ear lobe. Although I thought it was very strange gesture, I said nothing.

In spite of being extremely lonely during my two six-month sessions, I was introduced to mature things. I also reflected on how hard Dad worked and wanted us to succeed in life. Therefore, when I heard that my brother flunked his first year of medical school, I wrote him a castigating letter about wasting a year and not appreciating Dad's efforts. (He successfully repeated one year). The two sessions gave me only one year of high school credit because I failed to complete an assigned summer project of identifying, drawing, and mounting fifty weeds.

High School

MY MOST PLEASANT remembrances of high school involved the usual activities such as gymnasium, track, plays, and oratory. Some less worthy endeavors were periodic trips to Red Lake Falls for an occasional beer and the usual pranks of young teenagers.

One summer day several of my buddies and I were apprehended stealing edibles from the grouchy owner of a small commercial garden. In court, the judge sentenced the frightened culprits to work in the strawberry gardens. This, however, was terminated because we were devouring the profits. I was fearful that my father would come down hard on me. Surprisingly, he appeared more amused than angry.

One fall day we desperately wanted to attend an important Prowler football game at nearby Warren, Minnesota. The Model T transportation, an essential element for the trip, was in need of a tire replacement. Desperately we scoured the town and were finally able to steal one from behind the undertaker's parlor.

I fondly recall other high school experiences. Mr. Claffey, the pepper-haired school principal who was very strict about promptness, called me on the carpet on two occasions. On a beautiful spring day, I, along with Eudora and Art Swanson, my neighbor friend and sportsman, who also admired Eudora, played hooky. We canoed several miles down the river for a picnic. I answered the principal's inquiries as to why I had been absent by stating, "It was too beautiful a day to be in school." My good school marks apparently obviated discipline. However, during the next visit to explain my tardiness, he appeared quizzical to the fabricated explanation, "I had to help my father repair his instrument sterilizer." (Actually, I had overslept)

Then of course, there was the senior prom, which was the climax of our life with high school friends and the dawn of our future careers. A personal and embarrassing incident occurred during the dance. While I was dancing with the most sensual and exotic senior female, I developed an erection that necessitated me to walk back to my chair in a crouched position to detract visible detection. After the dance, my buddies and I were able to borrow a car and venture to nearby Red Lake Falls for a beer party. None of us had dates. The memory of Eudora, who had graduated the previous year, prompted my jealously when I saw her with a pimply-scarred senior.

Quasi-Military

THE SUMMER FOLLOWING my senior high school year, I happily for-
feited doing farm work by entering CMTC (Civil Military Training
Camp) at Fort Snelling, Minnesota. There was no objection from my
father. My adaptation to military life was easy because of Dad's home
discipline. Discipline at Snelling consisted of drills, proper backpack
wrapping, five mile marches, correct barrack cot making, and dress inspection. Officer barrack inspection was very thorough; the room had
to be spotless and cots had to be properly made, having a very tight
bouncy-top blanket. The uniform inspection was finished by observing our mirror-like shoeshine. A despicable kitchen duty, however, was
K.P., which consisted of washing large pots and pans and eating uten-
sils, in addition to peeling potatoes and waiting tables. Another duty
not appreciated was the lonely night guard duty. If one were caught
sleeping, he would be assigned devious chores, such as K.P.

Nor did we appreciate endless tasks of cleaning our World War I
rifles. Because they had been preserved in a smelly mess of Vaseline-like
Cosmolene, the rifles persistently seeped during the hot days. Early
bugle revelry was detested, as was early morning roll call and calis-
thenics. Following these activities was company inspection of the entire grounds. Every minute piece of debris was picked up. Rifle target
shooting would have been enjoyable if it had not been followed by
machine gun practice.

We were under the auspices of enlisted personnel—officers and
staff sergeants. All recruits were issued military dress, namely private
uniforms, fatigues, and shoes. Once, after I had been appointed to a
coveted position in an officer's quarters, I was harshly rebuked when I
reported in a partially soiled uniform.

There were some positive aspects of the military experience. We

76

looked forward to "titty time," a mid-morning break from drill at which time we each received a pint of cool milk. In general, the food was adequate and satisfactory. Above all, I was free from the disciplined farm work. At the end of the six-week period, we were each asked to sign up for the reserves. Very few accepted.

Farm Work and a Respite

I SOMETIMES WONDER IF our disciplined farm work was part of Dad's agenda for the preparation of our future. Or was it a means to have distinct control of us? During our teenage and pre-med summers, Galen and I worked on the farm. Jack escaped some of it by not succeeding in college.

While practicing in Grygla, Dad made frequent trips to the farm to supervise our austere work schedule, which was regulated by the following orders: "Clean this area of stones, use the stone boat to pile at certain spot, fence in those areas, summer fallow this area in order to hinder quack grass growth, mow this alfalfa field, windrow it, stack it into piles, stack hay, layer it with poles, apply salt and scrape the sides of the haystack to allow runoff, keep these forty acres clear of white and yellow clover by pulling them out one by one, and remove all the mustard from the oat field." Clearing grain fields of mustard hand-pulling was not a coveted job.

Our work force consisted of Galen, four years my senior, and Jack, two years younger. All through the teen years, we worked six days a week. During the summer, Jack and I stayed with the renter family where we were well-fed and kindly treated. I wondered why my father paid them money every month. It was a kind of summer foster home.

In 1931, when Dad was 61, he married his long-term nurse, Alice Solem, age thirty-five. We then moved back to Thief River Falls, where his farm trips were less frequent. Our enthusiasm for the close of the school year was markedly diminished, knowing of impending farm work. We expected an interval of teenage freedom before being transferred to the farm; however, we were shocked out of the hope when early the next day after the end of the school year, Jack and I were awakened with the order, "Pick up your duds and immediately head

78

for the farm." I once questioned his reasoning for this immediate post-school transfer. He advised us that he did not want us spending our time hanging around downtown. We packed our things, got into the Model T Ford, and along, with our work schedule, left for the farm.

One summer, however, we had a few weeks of respite. Dad always wanted to return to West Virginia to visit his birthplace, located up in the hills of Wayne County. He asked Jack and me to accompany him and his second family. In no way would we spend any time in the presence of our ill-behaved half-brothers. We so informed our father, and after no further discussion, he arranged for us to stay on the grounds of a former Goodrich friend who owned tourist cabins near Deadwood, South Dakota. He gave us one hundred dollars, and with that fortune we headed west in the Model T Ford. We borrowed a tent and two army cots and made camp near one of the cabins. We met the owner, Mr. Vaughan, who was very friendly, his wife, otherwise. Mr. Vaughan delighted in the amusement he received by telling tourists wild, fabricated western stories.

We found a beautiful pool up in the hills. Even though we were unable to catch any of the visible trout, we had fun swimming and diving. One day, as a tourist family stood by watching us, one of the girls commented on our graceful diving. "Where did you learn to dive?" she asked. I quickly answered, "We're pearl divers." Jack looked very bewildered and then said, "Yea, pearl divers." Fortunately, they asked no more questions.

We were in South Dakota for the yearly celebration of "Deadwood Days." During that time gambling was allowed. Fascinated by the roulette wheel, I put ten cents on a number, which returned eighty cents. We went to an outside activity where I asked a girl to dance. When she wondered what I was doing there, I told her we were with our father who was prospecting for gold. She obviously knew I was fabricating. An exceptionally dry year, forest fires were not that far away, and there was a grasshopper infestation. During our round trip, we became expert at changing tires and patching inner tubes; I counted fourteen tire changes. It was necessary for us to buy a new tire, and even though our trip took over three weeks, we were able to return with ten dollars.

In the meantime, my father was able to find the log cabin where he was born. When they first arrived in the vicinity of his birth, his inquiries were first met with reservation and disinterest. After he had introduced himself, they said, "You mean you are Charlie Adkins from up north?" The atmosphere abruptly changed, and they became overwhelmed with assistance and guidance. The Adkins family must have been prolific, because according to Dad's account, the family-named members could carry the county vote. He later told me that our decision not to accompany him was wise because the trip was not very pleasant. The enjoyment of the visitation of his boyhood home was overshadowed by the constant and undisciplined antics of his two young sons.

BOOK III

Medicine

Brothers

DAD WANTED HIS three sons to be doctors so he could have an Adkins' Clinic. He was successful with two, but not the third. He told everyone that Jack, his favorite, was going to be the surgeon. While Galen and I followed his orders, Jack dropped out of pre-med.

Instead, my youngest brother joined the Navy, and after an honorable discharge he went to a trade school. Later he developed a successful refrigeration repair business. He continued with his expletive vocabulary and for a while was somewhat abusive of alcohol. He was, however, a very beloved father until he died at age sixty-five of prostate cancer. My other brother Galen, after medical school, interned at the Detroit Henry Ford Hospital. At the end of his internship, he was offered a residency in urology. He too, chose another plan. He got married and returned to Grygla where he practiced for several years, utilizing the old hospital as his office and home. He later purchased a medical practice in Pine River, Minnesota. After an initial practice there, he lost his license because of alcoholism and Demoral addiction. He also lost his wife from a narcotic overdose. After making a remarkable recovery from the addiction to nicotine, alcohol and narcotics, he became the administrator of a mental institution in Cambridge, Minnesota. For his innovative work, he received a reward presented to him in Washington D.C. His previous lifestyle, especially nicotine addiction, precipitated his premature coronary death at age fifty-five. He was a very kind, compassionate and gracious person. There was only standing room at his funeral. He respected our father and was grateful for his education, but he was also at times bitter. He never showered Dad with accolades.

Early Introduction

URING THOSE VERY young years, I would hang around Dad's office and play in the yard in front of the hospital to keep an eye out just in case he had to leave on a call. Although I was an only four-and-a-half years old, I remember his sitting me upon a shelf while he interviewed patients. Years ago, country doctors made house calls. Rarely did a woman give birth in a hospital unless complications were indicated. I loved to go with him on regular calls. When he was treating the patients or visiting the farmers' livestock, I was invariably treated to a dish of bread, sweet cream and sugar. In later years, I would accompany him on collecting calls. He never sent bills, since there was no health insurance. It cost $2.00 for an office call, $25.00 for a confinement, $25.00 for a tonsillectomy, and $50 for an appendectomy.

Years later, when home from medical school, I accompanied my father on an interesting house call. It intrigued me because of its unusual nature. On this misty evening, when my father and I entered the house, I saw two people sitting on the living room sofa. On another sofa at the end of the hall was a teen-age girl writhing and moaning and waving her arms. After a brief look at the girl, my father walked to the kitchen, took out his glass Bunsen burner, and heated a teaspoonful of water into which he dropped a pill. He then withdrew the solution into a small sterilized syringe and administered the liquid into the girl's arm.

After we left the house, I asked my father what was wrong. I thought it looked serious. Dad replied, "There wasn't anything wrong. I gave her an apomorphine shot. And after she's puked her damn guts out, she'll come out of her tantrum."

My first introduction to surgery, however, was at age nine. Dad brought me up to the operating room in order to "assist" in the amputation of ten frozen toes. It was necessary to scrub up for 10 minutes before putting on a sterile gown and gloves. This procedure had to be repeated because I inadvertently contaminated myself. Dad had administered spinal anesthesia. The patient's feet were pulled over the end of the table and sterile drapes were applied. The feet were then prepared, and a newspaper was placed on the floor beneath them. I sat to the left of my father and watched helplessly with folded hands while he promptly removed the black, shrunken toes. One by one he dropped them, like pieces of coal, on the paper below. I was a bit nervous and scared but I didn't want to show it. My father was one of the first doctors in the upper mid-west to utilize spinal anesthesia. He occasionally traveled to medical centers in order to update his techniques. Ether was the safest choice for general anesthesia, but it had a suffocating effect during induction, plus an intense post anesthetic nausea. He removed my tonsils and later my appendix with it, but I was always left with its nightmarish effect.

Chloroform was available, but used only for very brief procedures because of its life threatening potency. This anesthetic was kept in a brown bottle in order to protect it from ultraviolet light. It was one of the many items within his black "doctor's bag." Dad once told me he used chloroform during deliveries in order to minimize pain, and he surmised that it also had a relaxing effect on the uterine cervix. In later years when pentathol was utilized, Dad refused to use it in confinement cases because of the effect on the baby. He taught Mr. Johnson, the county agent, how to safely administer ether anesthesia.

Pre-Med

As for me, my future profession had been destined for many years. After high school graduation and before leaving for the University of Minnesota, I received definitive instructions: "You are to maintain a B average and then enter medical school in two years. Do you understand?" I turned down several college scholarships after being accepted to the University of Minnesota.

It was 1934, during the depression, thus making acceptance much easier than currently. Enrollment was a panicky experience for me. The enormity of Minneapolis with its colossal skyscrapers, plus scurrying students, and class and building assignments—to a country boy—presented a new world. Pre-medical requirements were the same courses as for engineering students; namely, heat, electricity, optics and mechanics. Mathematics, German and English were separate. In the pre-admission exam, I did exceptionally well in Algebra, but my English test was so low that I was put in non-credited sub-freshman English. I realized then I could not meet the "two year" edict.

After several weeks of class, with marked trepidation I discussed my predicament with the English teacher. Fortunately, he transferred me. Unfortunately, the next level of English was filled, so they moved me to a higher level. We were required, of course, periodically to write theme papers. On one occasion, he called me into his office to ask if I had plagiarized (I doubt that I even knew the meaning of the word). Basically, the story was about an individual walking along the street wondering what was happening in a lighted house. The main character goes on relating scenarios, some joyous, some otherwise. I also included the lights of the hospital. The teacher was impressed with my fictitious story.

At the end of the semester, the teacher stood in front of the class

86

with a term paper in his hand and an English grammar book in the other. He said, "This term paper has every possible grammatical error in the book. If I were to grade it on points, it probably would have broken a record; however, I passed the student and gave an "A" based on the story content." It was a story about my father. I remember sitting in my room until the wee hours of the night without thought of grammar, only the true story of a country doctor.

Grades were sent to parents. I was meeting a "B" standard, except for optics in which I received a "D." Dad demanded an explanation. He seemed satisfied after I told him about my utter confusion about the subject. Actually, I was overjoyed about the passing grade "D." I studied diligently in order to meet his edict of a "B" average.

I was amazed and concerned about a premed student in my rooming house. This unusual individual spent most of his time lying in bed thinking out a formula to trisect a triangle. If I had a difficult problem with a higher algebra question, he would simply solve it in his head after I read him the question. Since he was of German heritage, apparently, he liked German class, which was the only one he attended. His farm parents became very disappointed when they learned of his expulsion.

The rooming house presented me with other new experiences. It was there where I first saw a tuxedo. Across the street from the house and my study window, I observed the fraternity brothers all dressed up in tuxedos on their way to a party. Other experiences during my rooming house days were more exciting. It was there where I first saw "the elephant." One day, one of the older roommates took several of us to accompany him to the "red light district" at Seven Corners in Minneapolis. When we first arrived in one establishment, we all refused female accommodations. In order to entice us, however, the Madame asked if we wanted to see a show. I first envisioned a naked diaphanous dressed female performing an exotic dance. Instead, we were led into a room where two prostitutes were engaged in oral sex. While they were performing, an engineering student in our group kept patting a glistening white thigh of the spread eagle prostitute, all the while offering encouraging words. Soon after the clitoral lingual stimulation, the receiving partner entered into an eye opening orgasmic response. Aside from pictures viewed out of Dad's anatomy book, that was the first live vagina I had ever seen. Furthermore, I learned that there was such a thing as oral sex.

At a later date, our next visit to another establishment was more intimate. After paying two dollars, I succumbed to an enticing experience: I bedded a young prostitute. During the raising and lowering process, I wanted to kiss her but was quickly rebuffed by her stating, "No one kisses me except my boyfriend, and I don't want my hair messed up." Afterwards, she triumphantly told the girls that it was my "first time." Whether we were all satisfied as we left remains a remote question.

In spite of long study hours, there was time for a few extra curricular activities made possible by the large city of Minneapolis. Cheap season tickets allowed us to attend Gopher football and basketball games. We anxiously followed away football games on the radio. All of us cheered when the Gophers won the national championship by beating Pittsburgh when Bernie Berman (Gophers' coach) moved tackle Ed Widseth to fullback. He scored the winning touchdown.

Having access to the swimming pool and handball courts, we toughened our palms. Everyone became quite adept at handball, especially Hans, the short-term German student. Occasionally on Sundays a five-cent streetcar ride would take us downtown Minneapolis to attend a fifteen-cent movie matinee. Forty to sixty-cents more would give us a full course dinner.

Sometimes we would imbibe. While we would have an occasional beer, hard liquor was seldom consumed. On one occasion, three of us became extremely intoxicated by visiting various bars. Exotic drinks— pink ladies, whiskey sours, Tom Collins and Bloody Marys—were entirely new to us. After asking a polite policeman for directions, we staggered back to the rooming house where the sink, the toilet and the bathtub received our exploding gastric contents. For many hours, it was a scenario of three nauseous, ailing, dumb students.

The freshman year of medical school was extremely challenging, especially anatomy. We had to know all the muscles of the body, their origin, insertion, function and nerve supply, plus all of the major blood vessels and their branches. It was necessary to be able to draw the cervical, brachial, and sacral nerve plexus along with their division into the peripheral nerves. All of the body bones with their respective muscle and ligament attachments had to be identified. The skull bones and sites of exit of the cranial nerves were included.

The learning process was enhanced by cadaver dissection—two students to each formaldehyded body. At the first presentation, I was somewhat fretful, too proud, however, to demonstrate my fragility. The anatomy department usually obtained unclaimed bodies from the city morgue. The excess formaldehyded bodies were hung up by large ear tongs and strung on racks similarly seen in a dry cleaning establishment. During the depression years, as opposed to later years, bodies were plentiful.

Shortly, we were introduced to a new and difficult terminology requiring intensive memory challenges. As an aid, most students utilized limericks to memorize all the cranial nerves: "On old Olympus' tiny top a Finn and German vend some hops" (Olfactory, Optic, Trigeminal, Trocheal, Abducens, Facial, Auditory, Glosophyarangeal, Vagus, Spinal Accessory, and Hypoglossal). There was another for the eight carpal wrist bones: "Never lower Tillie's pants; Mother might come home." (Navicular, Lunate, Triquetral, Pisiform, Greater Multangular, Lesser Multangular, Lunate, and Hamate.)

Gross anatomy, the study of body parts, was more mechanical. I was intrigued with developmental anatomy (embryology) which reveals the gradual transformation into the body from three germ layers of the fertilized ovum: ectoderm, mesoderm and endoderm. To illustrate: the skin and eyes come from ectoderm, the bones and muscles from mesoderm, and viscera from the endoderm. This intricate process can be interfered with by genes, disease, drugs, alcohol and idiopathic factors. Consequently, miscarriage, brain function or various congenital deformities can occur.

Because of low tuition and meager living expenses, I was able to attend college on my father's fifty dollar a month Spanish American Veteran's check. (As a contrast, present day yearly expenses—living and tuition—equal forty to sixty thousand dollars.) To save on the five-cent streetcar fare, we would frequently walk downtown. During my pre-medicine and the four years of medical school, I did buy a pair of three dollar Tom McCann shoes and a wrap-around winter coat. Books were mainly inexpensive. One time Dad sent me forty dollars to buy a prized three-volume set of *Spaltaholz Anatomy*. To help with expense I, like many students, was able to get a part-time job as a waiter in the university's dining room.

Fraternity Life

A<small>T MY BROTHER'S</small> insistence, I joined a fraternity—Phi Rho Sigma (Theta Thou Chapter). I accepted a pin from this group because the rushing was low-keyed and appeared more genuine than the other fraternities. There was no "hazing." I heard of previous hazing techniques. An oyster would be tied to a string that the person had to swallow. It was then pulled out and the process repeated. Another example: Two initiates would be blindfolded and ordered to urinate on one another. If one or the other refused, warm water would be squirted on one, making his opposite companion urinate in response.

We slept and studied within the frat house. Sound sleeping in the dorm room could be accomplished only after considerable periods of adjustment to the young adult night noises. During meals, I had never noticed Emily Post manners. Later, my brother Galen's advice to join a fraternity to learn social graces proved moot among all of the farting at the table. In general, fraternity life was serious. We had strict study rules, especially prior to comprehensives. Indeed, we did have few parties where "near beer" was spiked with alcohol, surreptitiously removed from the anatomy building.

Two students shared a room. I agreed to share with Joe Carlyle, who is long since dead. He was raised by his grandparents, apparently under very strict conditions. Because of his unsanitary habits, I became aware of why he was not a desirable roommate. He disliked soap and water. Before he went out on a date, we literally had to push him into the shower. He kept his used stockings in one drawer; and when a change was in order, he would pick each sock and match the pairs with the least odor. Our room was just above the street leading down to the nurses' dormitory. When he would hear the nurses walking by, he would get up from his desk, pull at his hair, wave his arms and yell, "I can't stand it! I can't stand it!" One particularly warm spring evening, he simply got up and left. He returned with a satisfied look on his face. His response to my question was, "I just came back from Seven Corners,"

His study habits were unique. Every available space except my desk was covered with open books and papers. Also, he would stand up and walk around, back and forth. Periodically, he would scratch away on his violin. He disliked my pipe-smoking; and after I quit, he once told me he had once stuck the stem up his ass. After his army service, he was relieved of his surgical residency because of his very slow pace in the operating room. He then entered the Army and went into plastic surgery.

At that time, most fraternities were segregated. The Phi Rho chapter did not "rush" or admit Jews. I became aware of this policy when I was told by a senior fraternity brother not ever to invite my very good friend Bill Harris over to the fraternity house again because he was Jewish. While I didn't know if he was or not, I told them if he wasn't welcome then I would leave. Nothing more was ever said. Bill was the most knowledgeable and intelligent person that I have ever met. I heard later that he had died of a brain tumor. Years hence as an alumnus, I visited the fraternity house where I saw an ethnic mixture.

Within the fraternity, I learned a few social graces. I found out there was such a thing as a topcoat. One cool evening, when leaving on a "rushing," I was asked, "Where's your top coat?" I deceptively replied that I had left it in the rooming house. They borrowed one for me, and I then knew what a top coat was. Moreover, while attending a banquet in St. Paul, I first saw and learned what a Demitasse cup was. After I took one gulp I asked, "Why would anyone serve coffee in such a tiny cup?"

Courtship and Marriage

While I was in pre-med, I came home for Christmas and decided to visit Eudora's parents, even though at that time we had no relationship. For old times' sake, I decided to buy her a Christmas present. I went to Montgomery Ward and put two dollars down on a small radio. The balance of nineteen dollars was to be paid by installments. I left the packaged Christmas present with her parents and, sometime later, I received a thank you note.(The radio still works and remains in my cabin at Waskish, Minnesota.) When I went back to the university, I was able to contact her, and thereby renew our romance.

Earlier Eudora desperately had wanted to go to a university, but her poor parents could not send her. After graduating from high school, she went to Lake Kabatogama in northern Minnesota to help her married cousin in a restaurant and beer joint. There she fell in love with a fellow, but after refusing an offer for marriage, she returned home. She then borrowed a few dollars from her father and entered a beauty school in Minneapolis.

My life with Eudora soon became permanent. After finishing beauty school, she got a position in Alexandria, Minnesota. Finding work frustrating, she decided to go to New York, where she took an apprenticeship as a laboratory technician at St. John's Hospital in nearby New Jersey. After corresponding, I had visited her when I was a fellow in anatomy at the University of Minnesota. While I was in New Jersey, we decided to get married. On our wedding night, we dined and danced at an eating-place where Frank Sinatra was singing. She worked at St. John's hospital as a laboratory technician for two years, returning to Minneapolis as I was finishing my senior year.

Medical students and their families often had financial problems. Our jobs with small salaries barely got us through. She got a ten-hour a day job at fifty dollars a month as a laboratory technician and secretary for a prominent obstetrician and gynecologist. While interning, I managed to rent a very cheap apartment on her fifty dollars and my seven-dollar and fifty-cent monthly salary. After my internship, she agreed to go along with my one-year acceptance of pathology fellowship. She gave up her job and accepted better pay and shorter hours as a technician with a prominent St. Paul internist. With her new seventy-five dollar per month salary and my fifty-dollar per month check, we were able to rent and live in a very nice St. Paul apartment.

Medical School

EVERY YEAR OF medical school was interesting. After the freshman year, I was offered a fellowship in anatomy, where I did research and assisted in teaching medical and nursing students. Before I accepted, I obtained clearance from my father. Unlike previous years, our senior year was very easy. We had clinical and laboratory work with fewer lectures. Excursions to a St. Paul brewery allowed us to have some free beer.

In 1936, one hundred and thirty of about three hundred and fifty applicants were accepted into the medical school. The most challenging parts of the curriculum were the comprehensive final examinations and the third year of medical school, in particular. During this year, we had eight hours of lectures, five days a week and four hours on Saturday morning. At the end, there was one week of study without class, followed by one week of terrifying written examinations in both morning and afternoon sessions.

Comprehensive meant an examination of all subjects taken in the previously nine months. Prior to the both sessions, bathroom privileges were permitted. In the first morning session, there was a frenzy of fright, exemplified by retching and vomiting by some students. No bathroom privileges were granted in the four-hour sessions. If a student flunked one course, he could repeat it, and then return the next year. However, two failures meant repeating the entire year. One of my fraternity brothers repeated the junior year three times and another one repeated the freshman year two times. Both did finally graduate, however. Comprehensive exams were discontinued some years later. I, too, had some academic problems. At the end of the junior year, I flunked an ear, nose and throat exam. It was the only school course I had ever failed.

During the senior year, we visited the St. Paul Bureau of Statistics, where we were able to review our birth certificates. To my amazement, my used name was not on my certificate. My father delivered me and in doing so, he inadvertently wrote his own name down twice. One for me as Charles Marion Adkins, plus his own as the attending doctor. Not remembering his error, he always called me Doug. Prior to leaving for the University of Minnesota, he told me my real name was Charles Douglas instead of Douglas Charles. I had always been called Doug. When I immediately informed him about his error, without any apology or any explanation, he had the birth certificate changed to *either* Charles Douglas Adkins *or* Douglas Charles Adkins. I chose to use Charles Douglas out of respect for my father, but yet, everyone still calls me Doug.

The summer after my third year, instead of going home I escaped farm work by accepting a junior internship at Swedish Hospital in Minneapolis. There we received board and room and a small pittance for doing required histories and physicals, starting IVs and performing periodic catherizations. By studying hard, I received an A in the repeat examination. However, for credit it was reduced to a B. At that time, I experienced a frightening incident. A patient on the third floor had not been attended by his physician for several days. In desperation, a nurse asked me to see him. He was having trouble breathing and, not knowing what to do, I administered intravenous aminophyline. After the treatment, I realized I had misinterpreted the usual dose; he had received five times the required amount. I dashed away, but I came back later to see him. Wondering if he was still alive, I was surprisingly greeted with these words, "You sure are a good doctor, I haven't felt this good for a long time." Little did he know.

During that summer interval, things other than medicine were on my mind. I started to listening to classical music suggested by Eudora's letters from New Jersey. She made me cognizant of great composers such as Bach, Beethoven and Mozart. Meanwhile, I had one evening with a nurse, and in the moonlight, I became quite passionate. Fortunately, she refused my feeble attempts at intercourse.

Internship

TOWARDS THE END of our senior year, there was a rush of excitement to apply for the long awaited internship; at last we could wear a white coat and carry our badge—the stethoscope. Minneapolis General Hospital was my first choice, excellent, because there an intern was given considerable responsibilities; namely, patient care, writing orders and even permission to write a few non-narcotic outpatient prescriptions. Because of the war, the usual two-year internship was cut to one year. We received seven dollars and fifty cents per month, along with long hours and starchy food. Supervision was carried out by the attending staff, the three-year specialty residents, and outside consultants.

During this time, I recall several significant incidents. The first day on the pediatric ward, I was bothered by the cacophony from multiple infants and children. The head nurse told me I would soon get used to it. She was right. There I had my first introduction to child abuse. A very thin two-year-old boy had been admitted. Proper nutrition and loving care had transformed him from a frightened emaciated child, to a happy, friendly little boy. I later learned that on the day of his discharge, he cried and struggled against leaving the hospital.

Blood transfusions were given in small increments. After I had transfused a small amount to an anemic infant, I returned the remaining blood to the bank. I then became aware that I had administered the wrong type. I broke down and confessed to the nurse; fortunately, there was no reaction because it was type "O"—universal type. It could have been fatal.

Psychiatric cases disturbed me, especially when I first saw a patient with delirium tremors. It took three orderlies to subdue him. Also, I observed a fifty-year-old man who was diagnosed as Senile Dementia. Yes, I was told it could happen to people that young. (It's now called

96

Alzheimer's disease.) There was an elderly man in a ward bed who to-day undoubtedly would be diagnosed with Alzheimer's. At one time he must have been in prison because, instead of calling out for a nurse or an orderly, he would ask for the warden. Occasionally, his face and hair would be spotted with feces, and one time I saw him try to drink out of his urinal. Two unmanageable sisters, who were diagnosed as schizo-phrenics, were held in a locked room. Since at this time lobotomy was passé, this severe treatment was not performed.

While my memory for patients' names is a bit lacking, I distinctly remember one name—Vladamer Vorbonoff. Why? Because when he immigrated to the United States, he permanently left his family in the old country. This so shocked me that his name was imprinted in my mind.

While on the medical service, I had my first experience with now well-known diseases. I frequently saw patients suffering from rheu-matic fever and valvular heart disease with failure. I remember a young female patient who was dying from sub-acute bacterial endocarditis. Some septic emboli broke off from the thrombotic damaged valve and spread throughout the body via the blood stream. At that time, with no antibiotics, death was inevitable. New diagnostic tools were being introduced. Now a common procedure, the EKG was just being inno-vated. The initial machine was large and burdensome. Digitalis was the only heart medicine available, nor do I recall that salt restriction was advised in patients with heart failure.

During that year (1941 to 1942) the number of obstetrical cases had dramatically subsided. Consequently, my bedside obstetrical ex-perience was limited: doing rectal examinations for determination of cervical dilatation, evaluating fetal heart tones, and observing an epi-siotomy, if indicated, and then watching the final expulsion of the pla-centa in order to examine it for complete expulsion.

I had some interesting experiences while I was working in the out-patient department. One was a not-so-humorous incident. Each week we put on a new, freshly-laundered white jacket. As I was bending over, doing an examination on a male infant, he urinated all over my fresh coat. Sitting nearby, his mother laughingly said, "I just knew he was going to do that." Not laughing, I finished the exam without the jacket. Also, while working in the outpatient, I was admonished by

Dr. Pollard—the not-so-well liked administrator—for refusing to do a physical examination. This particular individual was to have a non-emergency examination. I refused to do so until she had bathed herself, in order to abolish the dirt and stench. In fact, I gave her a nickel for a bar of soap.

When rotating on the surgical service, I witnessed my first serious post-operative problem. I saw an extensive abdominal evisceration, resulting in a gaping incision. The attending surgeons simply pulled it together with large strips of adhesive tape. As I feared, it didn't heal and the patient later succumbed. (Present day use of hyperalimentation with maintenance of a positive nitrogen balance now facilitates repair and healing.)

Most major surgeries were done by the attending surgeons or the senior surgical resident if he were competent. The intern on the surgical service occasionally was allowed to do an appendectomy, but only under the supervision of the senior resident. Once I had that opportunity, but the resident "took over" because I was blundering my way.

Every week we saw indigent patients in the outpatient clinic. Sexually transmitted diseases such as syphilis, gonorrhea, and herpes were common. Psoriasis, skin sores from scabies and bites from bedbugs were prevalent. Body lice were ubiquitous.

Our teacher for these serious problems was a very prestigious Minneapolis dermatologist who boosted the largest practice in the Twin Cities. I was impressed by his rapid diagnosis, but equally unimpressed by his aggressive and almost humiliating manner. The age and gender of the patient didn't matter: "Don't just stand there, open your pants and stick it out," he would sarcastically say. Some of the victims would be on the verge of breaking down. He appeared to get delight from his antics and insults. Many of us interns actually felt embarrassed. In no way did I aspire to be a wealthy dermatologist. As a matter of fact. in my entire school career I don't recall anyone ever teaching bedside manner.

We rotated through the very busy emergency room, often riding the ambulance. On a misty and rainy night, I was along on a DOA (Dead on Arrival). With lights flashing and sirens screeching, the ambulance sped non-stop to the call where a screaming mother stood surrounded by the police. Inside lay a dead teenage boy. He had committed suicide by putting a bullet through his head. The bullet shattered his skull with such force that brain tissue was spattered all over the wall. He first had fired a practice shot, then inscribed a note: "You didn't think I would do it, did you?" While the police and ambulance drivers were making their reports, I stood by helplessly.

Many of the ambulance drivers were seasoned veterans, while the interns that accompanied them were young and inexperienced. On a very hot summer day while I was riding in an ambulance, we were forced to walk up three flights of stairs in an old apartment house to attend a young woman who had had a miscarriage. I instructed the drivers to place her on the stretcher. Instead, they said, "Doc, she is ok, she can walk." She stood up and immediately fell back in bed due to hypotension from blood loss. They quickly placed her on the stretcher and "rewarded" her by carrying her down the three flights of stairs. On occasion, we had to attend inmates in the county jail. While walking past the cells, we were greeted by cups being banged on the bars, accompanied by pleas for cholorohydrate (the knockout medication).At the end of my internship, I again encountered the incompetent Dr. Pollard. Having just bought my army uniform, I was about to report to Carlisle Barracks. Not knowing how long the war was going to last, I wanted to say goodbye to my seventy-three-year-old father. Since I was on anesthesia rotation with only one week left in my internship, it was possible to get another intern to cover for me. After I explained the situation to Dr. Pollard, he refused my request for a week off. When I responded that I was going without his permission, he retorted, "I am not going to give you your internship credit." I disregarded his warning and I went home to visit my father. I did, however, receive intern credit.At times in my school education, I , myself, had physical problems. During my junior and senior years of internship, I again had several attacks of renal colic that required hospital admission to the university and the general hospitals. Also while interning, extensive diagnostic studies were done at Fort Snelling.

BOOK IV

Pathology

Post-Grad Training

AFTER INTERNSHIP, I felt in need of further medical knowledge. Therefore, I accepted a one-year fellowship in pathology under Professor Dr. Tom Bell at the University of Minnesota. At that point, I no longer asked or needed parental guidance. My wife was in full agreement with my decision. Some fragility of the medical profession became apparent while I was in pathology.

I learned that cause of death wasn't one hundred percent evident. I observed a very preventable tragic case, wherein a family physician had operated on a middle-aged man with a pre-operative diagnosis of appendicitis. On autopsy, death was due to a ruptured cecum. The patient had a constricting cancer of the ascending colon, along with a non-functioning ileocecal valve. This allowed pressure to build up in the cecum, subsequently rupturing and producing fatal fecal peritonitis. Surgery for such a cancer by an experienced surgeon would be relatively easy with a good chance of cure. This gave me more impetus for further training and study.

I remember other cases as well, such as untimely deaths due to ruptured cerebral aneurysm and sudden death from pulmonary embolism. Early ambulation has now markedly reduced venus thrombosis and embolic syndrome. That year of pathology fellowship brought into prospective the ubiquity of life and death.

Occasionally, the pathology fellows did coroner cases at the city morgue for five dollars each. That included the trip to the morgue, entire autopsy, weighing and microscopic examination of each organ, and dictation and etiology of death. In many cases, death was grossly evident, caused by accidents or weapon deaths.

I remember two more interesting coroners' cases. During a marital altercation, a husband suffered fatal head injuries administered by his

103

wife's hammer blows. A more enlightened case produced humorous audience response. It was determined that the cause of death of an octogenarian was a myocardial infarct that took place during intercourse with a young female partner.

Local hospitals made an effort to obtain a certain percentage of autopsies in order to maintain the required quotas. These were usually done by the hospital's own pathologist. Each week, a very productive conference would be held. Attending University of Minnesota pathologists, along with other pathologists from Minneapolis and St. Paul, would present clinical cases, accompanied with challenging microscopic slides.

Dr. Bell had a great sense of humor. As we stood by, he would cut up specimens for microscopic study, which had been sent to him from family practitioners outside of the University of Minnesota. He once held up a small jar containing some liquid and stool fragments and asked us to identify the intestinal parasite. We were all silent. Chuckling, he told that this was from someone who had eaten a lot of grapefruit. Another time he was quite grim when he showed us a lump of breast tissue that had been removed from a pre-menopausal girl. (I often wondered if she questioned why her adult breasts were not the same). Dr. Bell once told us that we wouldn't be a seasoned pathologist until we had done an autopsy on a "floater." (a body that had been autopsied after it had been removed from days or weeks in the water).

Dr. Bell was most gracious. I always felt welcome in his office while going there for a microscopic consultation. He loved cigars. I was reminded of the aroma when my father occasionally smoked cigars. Tragically, soon after he retired, Dr. Bell was killed in a car accident.

Following the pathology year, a decision about my future had to be made. Dad wanted me to join him in Thief River Falls. Eudora, who didn't care for my father, informed me that if I accepted the offer, she would not go with me. She said I would in essence be a puppet, which would destroy me. I wanted to be a family physician, however, but realized further training, especially in surgery, was imperative.

My Mentor—Doctor Maxiener

FOLLOWING MY FELLOWSHIP in pathology, I was offered a pediatric residency. I turned down that offer to pursue the necessary surgical training. I heard that a highly skilled and respected surgeon, Dr. Stanley Maxeiner , was looking for an apprentice.

Dr. Maxiener, well- respected by his peers, wrote several surgical papers, received several honors and was instrumental in initiating the Minneapolis Surgical Society. Its purpose was to raise the status of surgery in Minneapolis. I met him at the Asbury Hospital when I was doing an autopsy on a patient who had expired after undergoing a low colorectal anastomosis for a carcinoma. The patient had refused a colostomy and an abdominal perineal resection.

I went to Dr. Maxiener's home and was very impressed by his massive library. After considerable negotiation in which I wouldn't accept two hundred and fifty dollars a month, he agreed to three hundred dollars, but with no benefits. He presented the following work schedule: 1) assist him at the operating table 2) be in the office every afternoon six days a week 3) make hospital rounds every morning with him, after office hours, as well as personal rounds twice on Sundays and holidays, 4) be on call twenty-four hours every day 5) be available at all times for emergency calls for the express agency 6) make house calls when necessary, and 7) have his little bag of instruments brought to the respective hospitals ahead of time so it would be available for the scheduled operations. I would be allowed two weeks of paid vacation each year.

In five years, only once did I have a Saturday morning off. During one pheasant season, when I told him I enjoyed hunting, he said, "Fine, I'll arrange a Saturday hunt with Dr. McMann," a referring family doctor who lived in pheasant country near Green Isle, Minnesota. Initially, I was surprised and overjoyed until he qualified it by stating that I had to be back in the office by one o'clock. We hunted, with no success, until it was time for me to leave and make the office deadline. Graciously, however, he gave me a few days off in order to drive to Thief River Falls to assist in funeral arrangements for Eudora's father.

Dr. Maxiener also reminded me about how poor he had been and how hard he had worked while under the tutorship of Dr. Emitt Farr. His early pecuniary problems undoubtedly nurtured his parsimony.

Under his direction, Dr. Maxiener and his highly skilled mentor, Dr. Farr, wrote a small book on the technique of local anesthesia. I learned how to do head and neck surgery, plastic facial surgery, lip resection, tonsillectomy, thyroidectomy and brachial cyst removal. Other operations such as cholecystectomy, appendectomy and inguinal hernia repairs and extremity surgery were also done under local anesthesia. Prior to its administration, an intravenous would be started, along with a mild sedation of a narcotic. Included in the IV was atropine or scopolamine, the latter of which causes amnesia. Local anesthesia would rarely provoke vomiting. Dr. Maxiener would occasionally lecture to medical students about the advantage of this technique.

As an excellent teacher, he expected only perfection. Even though he had large hands, he was very gentle with tissue. His protuberant belly didn't prevent him from carrying an eleven handicap at a very prestigious Minneapolis golf club. During his training with Dr. Farr, just after WWI, anesthesia was performed with ether or local anesthesia.

While Dr. Maxiener's surgery was mainly exemplary, he like all surgeons was capable of making a mistake. Once while we were partner, he did a herniography on the mother of my good friend Dr. Utendorfer. During the hernia repair, Dr. Maxiener inadvertently tore the femoral vein. Dr. Utendorfer was called from a nearby waiting room into surgery where he repaired the vein laceration. Because of the possibility of thrombus formation in the femoral vein, the patient was placed on prophylactic IV heparin. Several days later, she suffered a brain hemorrhage, which caused complete aphasia and minor muscle paralysis.

If Dr. Maxiener's surgeries were invariably flawless, his penury never faltered. After the above-mentioned operation, Dr. Utendorfer was asked to come to the office. He was shocked by, instead of getting a statement of remorse; he was presented with a bill.

Another example of Dr. Maxiener's penury occurred shortly after our partnership had begun. A prominent attorney listed in Who's Who, had recurring peptic ulcer hemorrhage. His practice required overseas consultation, and after an episode of bleeding while in Italy, he later consulted Dr. Maxiener who allowed me to do a subtotal gastrectomy. After his first office visit, Dr. Maxiener summoned me into his office; and while smiling, held up ten brand new fifty-dollar gratuity bills. Secretly, I hoped for a portion, but to no avail. The attorney was never told who actually had done the surgery.

When I was under his apprenticeship, I experienced an extremely disturbing incident. We had a patient by the name of Lee Erickson, who developed a large pancreatic cyst. An accepted drainage procedure, anastomosing the cyst through the stomach walls was accomplished. However, because of the digestive properties of pancreatic juice, gastric mucosal ulceration produced repeated massive hemorrhages. During one such episode, I drove over seventy miles per hour from my home through town in order to do a cut-down for blood replacement. Most all of his veins had been traumatized by previous injections. After repeated episodes of hemorrhage, Dr. Maxiener finally performed a gastric resection.

Weeks of hospitalization completely depleted the patient's savings along with money from a new mortgage. His wife stayed at his bedside and would often sleep in the nearby bathtub. She later suffered from a lumbar disc syndrome. At the first office call, Dr. Maxiener confronted him about payment. He was not only a human shell of a man, but completely broke and out of a job. Although dismayed, but grateful that he was still alive, he never returned to Dr. Maxiener's office. Personally, I felt that money talk at that time was very inappropriate. As they left the office, my heart went out to them.

In 1953, I received American Board of Surgery approval after passing the written and oral examinations. Even though earlier I had rejected a partnership, I re-joined Dr. Maxiener as a partner because my wife and I were extremely poor. I went into partnership with him at 14% with 1.5% raise each year. To start a surgical practice would have required a certain amount of money, so I felt the best decision would be to join him.

After joining Dr. Maxiener, I had a very good relationship with him. I could now do my own cases; after a few years, I decided to go out on my own. We parted amicably. During my years with him, before and after, I learned many things about the practice of medicine and surgical privileges. Prior to and during the forties, family practitioners carried out some surgery. I was acquainted with one so called surgeon who had a very talented family doctor friend. He would scrub up and do surgery; in other words "ghost surgery." The patient never knew.

During those five years of servitude under Dr. Maxiener's teaching, I acquired techniques which were assets to my residency and career. I learned local anesthesia, gentleness of tissue, and composure and confidence in the operating room. He also advised, "You can do it, if you can see it." Following his advice, I read surgical journals, regularly attended surgical and hospital staff meetings, and kept very precise records. Of great importance, was a tip on bedside manner: if you are not pressed for time, sit down and visit with a patient.

My criticisms of Dr. Maxiener were few. I did not like the manner in which he settled his accounts with a referring physician who may or may not have assisted at the operating table. After several surgical cases, he would discuss their respective fees, while his private patients' small bills would be mailed. The individual larger fees would be presented to patients in his office, wherein, he would first read the esoteric surgical procedure and then quote an amount. That figure, however, would be considerably reduced if paid in cash. To me, such negotiations appeared to be bargaining over a human being. While I never was a participant, I heard these conversations from my adjacent office. Apparently, at that time it was the common way to discuss payments with referring physicians and patients.

At last, after four and one-half years of apprenticeship, I realized I wasn't ready or capable to do surgery. As an assistant, I was merely allowed to do abdominal closures. I enjoyed surgery, however, and while I admired Dr. Maxiener's skill, it appeared to me that hospitals would soon require qualifications before allowing surgical privileges. Therefore, I wrote to the American College of Surgeons to see if my year of pathology and four and one-half years of surgical apprenticeship would be adequate for entrance. They only allowed me one year of credit.

I remained under Dr. Maxiener's tutorship from 1943 until July, 1948. During the last two or three years, I was very frustrated. Being away from home most of the time, living in poor apartments, and having anxiety over a precarious marriage, I decided a change was necessary. The planned pregnancy, which had resulted in the birth of a healthy child, now four years old, didn't ease the frustration.

Earlier, I had been urged by our dentist and by Dr. Roscoe Webb, a very successful and excellent surgeon, to apply for a surgical residency. This residency, however, would require financial subsidies in order to support a home and family. Dr. Swanson, our dentist, promised to lend me money.

In the meantime, Dr. Maxiener wanted me to become his partner. Since our marriage was somewhat shaky, I felt if we could have our own home and a little more financial security we would then be more compatible. Upon his return from a Texas vacation, Dr. Maxiener demanded an answer about a permanent partnership. I was so certain he would accept my willingness to join him as a partner, we put a down payment on a house. My certainty was based on my input into the account, mainly house calls and referrals from my father, brother and classmates. The day after his return, we had a meeting in his office where I told him I had accepted the partnership, albeit I would be guaranteed a monthly stipend of one thousand a month. In a bellicose manner, he said, "I can't afford it!" Aware of his stinginess, I was prepared for a negative answer.

My answer was, "Fine, Dr. Maxiener, I am leaving for a surgical residency starting at the Veterans' Hospital under the auspice of the University of Minnesota." For the first time in about five years, he looked pale and shocked. He asked, "Why are you doing this?" I responded, "I want to become a surgeon, and I need to find out if I have that capacity. You have not allowed me to be tested, only to do all of the spinal anesthesia and closure of some of the abdominal incisions."

That day after our conference, I bought a pint of whiskey and Eudora and I celebrated. I had the bases covered.

Author, Dr. Douglas Charles Adkins

Apprentices: (Back row) Author, Dr. Bob Maxiner, Dr. Finklinburg, Dr. Mackenzie; (Front row) Dr. Caron, Dr. Stanley Maxiner, Dr. Hoftert

Author with future wife Eudora Hawkins, circa 1931.

Author in college days

Another Mentor, Dr. Hay

SINCE I DEFINITELY wanted to become a qualified surgeon, I visited Dr. Lyle Hay, a former fraternity brother of mine who was professor of surgery at the Veterans' Hospital. I asked him if there were possible surgical residencies available. Fortunately, I was able to begin on July 1, 1948, under the tutelage of Dr. Hay, who was well acquainted with Dr. Maxiener's technique since he was a consultant at the VA.

My residency at the VA hospital, which was under the auspices of the surgical department of the University of Minnesota, started July 1, 1948, and ended July 1, 1951. Just prior to that, a financial predicament arose. Our dentist, who had previously promised to lend us money, declined when I informed him of the residency acceptance. Since the residency paid two hundred dollars per month, it was obvious that mortgage and living expenses required a subsidy. Fortunately, we were able to obtain the amount from Eudora's mother. Because I was a member of the Hennepin County Medical Society, I was able to accept house calls from the medical exchange. Thus, when I was not at the hospital, I became available for emergency calls day or night. At five dollars a call, it helped.

Residents would do surgery under the supervision of attending staff or visiting consultants. Required rotation was made through various specialties such as neurological, orthopedic, plastic, and vascular. In all the areas there were post-graduate courses, lectures, papers research, and conferences. We periodically had "O.D." (overnight hospital coverage). The goal was to become chief surgical resident. In one week, I did seven gastric resections for peptic ulcer complications. As a chief surgical resident, one was on his own in the operating room unless consultation was requested.

I once called Dr. Lyle Hay, professor and chief of surgery, because I

113

was unable to dislodge a gallstone that was impacted in the lower end of the common bile duct. I was hesitant to open the duodenum and do a sphincterotomy of Oddi. Dr. Hay carried out a very simple maneuver by reflecting the duodenum, thus exposing the distal common duct. He then made an incision over the impacted stone, easily removing it. After surgery was over, I went into his office to thank him. He responded by thanking me for calling him in because he had recently read an article describing that particular technique. (It is of interest that several years later while in private practice I was called into an operating room by another surgeon to do the same procedure.)

In additional ways, I was grateful for Dr. Hay's influence. As a highly intelligent and skilled surgeon, he demonstrated humility. At the end of each day, we had surgical rounds at which time we would discuss all the problem cases. It was here I recognized Dr. Hay's bedside kind behavior. I was a bit taken back, however, by open and candid discussion in front of a patient who had been found to have inoperable cancer. I never observed an undue reaction in such cases. There was no whispering.

On another occasion, Dr. Hay demonstrated a very subtle but impressionable teaching reprimand to a surgical resident. The resident had explained his gall bladder and common duct exploration of that day. With this procedure, a drainage t-tube is most always left in the common duct for bile drainage. After Dr. Hay noticed the empty t-tube vial bottle, he simply walked over to the patient's bed, threw back the covers, and while peering at the chagrined and frightened resident, he calmly opened the t-tube clamp. Bile flow appeared, the message was received. Nothing more was said, even though peritoneal bile leakage is very serious. The resident confessed to me that he was fearful his residency would be terminated.

Years later, this subtle method of a teaching reprimand was of personal benefit to me, keeping me from losing my cool. During the early hours of the morning, I was informed that my post-operative intensive care patient had no urinary output. On the twenty-five mile trip to the hospital, even though I had been told all vital signs were normal, I was very concerned and bewildered. At the bedside, when I threw back the covers and traced the tubing from the bladder catheter to the bedside urine bag, I found a kinked tube. After this was straightened, immediately there was a healthy flow of urine. The two nurses, looking at me with wide eyes, waited for my response. While hiding my left clinched fist, I calmly said, "Always be certain that all tubes have free passage." I drove home for a few more hours of sleep with silent thanks to Dr. Hay's teaching.

The Residency

DURING MY RESIDENCY, several incidents remain impressive. At that time, there was no open-heart surgery. However, stenosis of the mitral valve would be dilated by inserting a finger between the stenotic valves. A purse string suture was placed in the left auricle. Following this procedure, a finger was put through the incision in the auricle, down through the stenotic valve. Bleeding was prevented by tightening the purse string. I observed this procedure being performed by Dr. Frank Johnson, who at that time was a resident in chest surgery. It was done under the supervision of an attending chest surgeon.

I was once asked to do a gastroenterostomy and vagotomy on a patient, utilizing only local anesthesia without any pre-op medication other than atropine. Because of the patient's severe emphysema, it was necessary to have him in a partial upright position. The local anesthesia itself was a challenge. When the patient developed hiccups, gastrointestinal sutures had to be inserted between each hiccup.

Several interesting episodes occurred during my early residency years. Vascular surgery was limited at that time. In selected cases, lumbar sympathectomy would be performed for peripheral limb ischemia. I was requested to do this in a patient under local anesthesia. Fortunately, since the patient was not obese, it went well. At the request of the same individual, I performed the identical procedure on the opposite side. At the VA, soapsuds enemas were always given in preparation for a proctoscopic exam. In one such procedure a patient's colon was ruptured. (It was the only case of soapsuds peritonitis that I have ever had). After aspirating the soapsuds, the colon was sutured and no complications occurred. I remembered the case very well because the patient's wife went home before the surgery stating, "He's a tough old bird and he will be ok." He was. Later I performed a radical mastectomy on an African American male, the only male I have ever seen with breast cancer.

While on the plastic surgery service, I vividly recall three third degree burn cases. Two young men returning from a pheasant hunting trip were badly burned when they stopped to pull out a driver who was trapped in a burning gasoline truck. The youngest nimrod, about twenty four years of age, was engaged to be married. He suffered severe head and body burns, which required multiple skin grafts. His nose, ears and face became severely burned, producing horrible deformity. After discharge from the hospital, his fiancé left him. I later heard he became an alcoholic. His friend had severe body burns but no facial burns. After multiple skin grafts, he was able to go home for Christmas. The suffering of severe burn cases is incomprehensible.

The third burn case offered me a different challenge. That young male and his friends were at a drinking party in celebration of his

upcoming marriage. While smoking in bed, he fell asleep, igniting the bed. He suffered third degree burns over the lower abdomen, the pubis and the dorsal two thirds of his penis. While waiting for further care and skin grafting, he signed out against advice. A few days after he returned, I grafted his penis and was able to fashion a mild pressure bandage. He did get married and I later heard that everything went well.

The VA hospital had few orthopedic emergencies, thus most of those operations were elective. During my rotation on that service, a vitalium cup hip joint replacement was the most challenging surgery I had during my entire residency.

One time during my orthopedic service, a nurse handed me an envelope with something a man had left for me. It contained a note of thanks and a hundred dollar bill (a bonanza). Some weeks previously, while I was on the vascular service, a patient who had long-standing peripheral edema due to previous femoral vein thrombosis approached me. He had carried disability insurance for many years and had been repeatedly refused compensation. After examination, he asked me to write a letter to the insurance company. I did so, they relented, and in appreciation, he sent me one hundred dollars.

As senior resident, I did one case, which suddenly boosted my ego. I was asked to see a patient with abdominal pain. On the physical examination, it was noted he had false teeth. His history revealed the night before he drank some martinis with toothpicked olives. A pre-operative diagnosis was made of peritonitis due to a toothpick perforation of the terminal ileum, and surgery confirmed it. (I had remembered an article about such a triad).

While at the VA, I was astonished about the plethora of secretaries. Invariably, they straightened up their desks before four o'clock at which time they would all be on the starting line, ready to leave. One morning, after I had been on O.D., I decided on a little humor. While sleepily arriving near one of the surgical secretary's desks, I was asked if I had been busy. "Yes," I replied. "Yesterday afternoon at exactly one minute to four there was an accident at the hospital door entrance." "Oh my! What happened?" I said, "Well, this very elderly male was almost crushed to death at the entrance by the entourage of exiting stenographers."

Incompetency

ONCE I HAD an experience that demonstrated three negative aspects of a particular doctor: avarice, total lack of knowledge of gentle usage of local anesthesia, and complete trust and admiration of the patient for the family physician.

To afford a brief vacation for Eudora and me, I used one week of my two-week respite allotment to work for a family physician. While assisting this doctor, I was asked to see a patient with an infected toenail, usually a foul-smelling condition. After finding a small-gauged needle and a clean syringe, hopefully sterilized, I gently infiltrated Novocain into the base of the big toe. Such a block requires a few minutes to produce anesthesia. Shortly thereafter, the doctor asked the toe owner how he was doing. The patient said, "It still isn't numb." The doctor's answer: "I'll fix that." Then he took a syringe of Novocain and, with a large needle, javelined it into the end of the big toe, causing a large cry of pain. The patient, with a condescending look at me, changed moods and said, "NOW it's numb." Then he turned an admiring gaze at *his* doctor. I stood by, saying nothing but thinking of Neanderthal methodology. It concerned me that he used the same syringe and needle for individual hypo injections, utilizing inadequate sterilization only with alcohol solution immersion.

Money was the most important part of this doctor's profession. He would see fifty to one hundred patients a day, which was an obvious method of culling for surgical cases. This augmented his income. A pleasing personality, plus a two-dollar office call, aided patient admiration. While obviously he had been granted some surgical privileges at Swedish Hospital, there was no knowledge of his surgical training. I never saw him at any of the Hennepin County Medical Society meetings.

I made seven house calls for which I was pledged five dollars a call, over and above the meager week's salary. This self-centered doctor wrote out a check, left it on his desk, but failed to give it to me. He built a new office and in order to preserve his bankroll, he lived there in a small partition. After impregnating his office nurse, he needed a home. Therefore, some living expenses, except the mortgage, couldn't be deducted from his income tax. Once he asked me to assist during a thyroidectomy, which he blundered through. I should have been tipped off because after the surgery he didn't mention an assistance fee, even though I would have accepted a lunch or a parking ticket. As I left his office after not receiving the house call check, his nurse looked at me and said, "I'm sorry." I was the sorry one.

BOOK V

Travails of a Surgeon

Local Anesthesia

DURING MY CAREER, most surgeons rarely used local anesthesia for major surgery. While not popular, this kind of anesthesia was an important aspect of my career. It was due to my mentor, Dr. Maxiener's influence. My ability to do local anesthesia was reminiscent of his teachings.

Helpful in my surgical practice were the following; utilization for thyroidectomy, bronchial cysts, thyroglossal cysts, hernias, cholecystectomies, skin lacerations (large and small), skin lesions and facial surgery. Also, subperitoneal infiltration was important to promote abdominal relaxation during a difficult abdominal closure or for some fractures such as colles (wrist). Local anesthesia was productive in other procedures. During thyroidectomies, it was necessary to allow the patient to speak in order to prevent injury to the recurred laryngeal nerves. In later years, thyroidectomies were done under general anesthesia with exposure of both the recurrent laryngeal nerves. More importantly, it was utilized whenever possible to prevent vomiting and aspiration in the presence of a full stomach or in some patients with respiratory problems. Several representative cases follow:

Aspiration is a very serious situation. I observed one death on the table in which Dr. Maxiener engaged the assistance of Dr. Ralph Knight, professor of anesthesia at the University of Minnesota. It involved general anesthesia for a gastric resection on a patient who had a bleeding peptic ulcer. As the intra-tracheal tube was being inserted, he vomited blood, aspirated and died.

At another time, a patient was brought to Methodist Hospital following a lightning strike incident. He had just finished a big dinner when lightning struck a tree adjacent to his cabin. The explosion penetrated him with wooden fragments. One splinter entered his neck from one side through to the other side, the other fragment penetrating the left maxillary bone just below the left orbit.

I suggested to the MD anesthesiologist that I could do the surgery under local anesthesia along with adjunctive intravenous Demoral. The doctor's refusal resulted in aspiration and two weeks of hospitalization in the intensive care unit for treatment of aspiration atelectasis pneumonia, a critical respiratory problem. Fortunately, neck dissection revealed no esophageal, tracheal, or blood vessel injury. The maxillary stick fragment was removed with difficulty with sterilized regular tool pliers. Local anesthesia could have easily been performed by cervical and facial nerve blocks.

Another aspiration case was at North Memorial Hospital in a patient who had an early perforation of a peptic ulcer. This also occurred as the intra-tracheal tube was being inserted. Because the perforation time was short, a decision was made to treat him conservatively with nasal suction and antibiotics. He did well.

Aspiration was prevented by utilizing local anesthesia in still another case. A nine-year old boy was admitted to St. Mary's Hospital after he had fallen off a clothesline apparatus. One of the line's hooks caught his left forearm, tearing off the flexor carpi ulnaris muscle. It was left hanging by its attachment to the pisiform carpal bone (wrist bone). The relatively large wound was grossly contaminated with dirt and grass. The boy had just finished his evening meal and obviously had a full stomach. To me, this was a definite indication for local anesthesia.

Before the operation, I noticed that the boy was very apprehensive; therefore, I tried to soothe him with some bedside manner. He was stoic and cooperative, but frightened. To approach the subject, I first told him that boys don't cry—just girls. I told him also I had a magic coin to be squeezed if he had any pain during the surgery. The forearm was easily anesthetized. Debridement was accomplished; but during closure, it was evident that the skin flap was not sufficient to cover the wound. The boy then informed me that when he looked up from the ground after the accident, he saw something hanging on the hook, which undoubtedly was a piece of his skin. A graft was then removed from the lateral side of his left thigh and sutured over the rest of the wound. When he once complained of pain, I told him to squeeze the coin harder. After it was all over, he asked me if that coin was really magical. I was honest with him, gave him the coin, and complimented his cooperation and fortitude.

A colleague of mine once had a male patient who continued bleeding following a tonsillectomy. Dr. John Clarke needed someone to come to Waconia Hospital to ligate the external carotid artery. I referred him to the excellent all-American board members at St. Louis Park Medical Clinic. Several days later, since bleeding had continued, he called to request that I come out and do the other side. I agreed only if the patient would accept local anesthesia. When we approached the patient, he first said no, but then relented after being told if he felt any pain except the initial needle prick, no fee would be submitted. We gave some intravenous Demerol, and ligation of the other external artery was done under local. After dictation, we went to his bedside, and he sleepily asked, "When are you going to operate?" My colleague informed me that during the previous operation, the patient had vomited blood during the insertion of the intra-tracheal tube. The aspiration caused intensive commotion among the entire operating room personnel.

In another case, this same doctor apologetically consulted on a Mrs. Arnold who had such a massive ovarian cyst it required her to breathe in an orthopnic (upright) position. Dr. Clarke was hesitant to call me because the anesthetist at the Waconia Hospital had refused administration of general anesthesia. Also, the patient had refused a transfer to another hospital. (Note: At that time, they didn't have M.D. anesthesiologists.) She willingly accepted local anesthesia. With her in a somewhat upright position and with oxygen administration, we made a xiphoid to pubic incision. Subperitoneal local infiltration produced total muscle relaxation; and at that point, the patient was told she would experience pain. There was no way to block the round and broad ligaments. Indeed, she had a short episode of pain at the time the massive cyst was lifted out of the peritoneal cavity. Local was then applied to the above ligaments, the twenty-pound cyst removed, the flaccid abdomen closed, and normal breathing vital capacity was restored.

I once scheduled a gastric resection on an eighty-year-old lady for a partially obstructing cancer of the pyloric portion of the stomach. Even though she was thin and would be an acceptable candidate for general anesthesia, she agreed to local. After the gastric resection, and as I was on my way out of the operating room, she took my hand, thanked me and asked, "Can I now eat potatoes?" Since the elevators were out of order, she agreed to walk one small flight of stairs. The nurses, however, disallowed it.

Another physician, Dr. Fred Walker, an excellent internist, asked for consultation on an elderly man with chronic lymphatic leukemia and acute cholecystitis. After much family persuasion, the man agreed to undergo surgery. Under local anesthesia, a cholecystomy was done with the removal of a gallstone and insertion of a cholecystostomy drainage tube. Ten days later, he went to a religious holiday event in Chicago.

In another case, local anesthesia also was used to do a cholecystectomy and removal of a one-inch ball-valve common duct stone in a lively eighty-year-old male. The family had been told that their granddad had fatal pancreatic cancer. They were just to keep him comfortable. Aside from weeks of intermittent jaundice, he didn't have the usual signs pathognomonic of pancreatic cancer such as pain, deepening jaundice, and weight loss. He made an uncomplicated recovery and returned to his happy family. Incidentally, most members of his family had been patients of my father.

Still another case involved mandatory local anesthesia. One evening, my partner, Dr. Buie, asked me if I could come to Fairview Hospital to perform an appendectomy under local anesthesia on the fifteen-year-son of a family practitioner. Alternate anesthesia (general or spinal) was impossible because the boy had such a severe vertebral deformity. Since his posture was almost fetal, it was necessary to approach the appendix through a lateral flank incision. Although the operation under local anesthesia went well, I was a bit apprehensive in front of the audience, namely the doctor, the nurse, the anesthetist, and the hospital anesthesiologist. The patient's post-operative course following the removal of a gangrenous appendix was uncomplicated.

Duties of Doctors

IN GENERAL, PHYSICIANS have an agenda: time for hospital rounds, conferences, departmental meetings, office hours, if applicable, the surgery schedule, and the unavoidable "on-call" schedule. Sometimes these many duties are compromised. Inevitable interruptions frequently take place; for example, phone calls during office hours. (Currently, they are intercepted and carefully analyzed by the doctor's nurse assistant before referral to the physician.) A doctor also must accept being called away from home at important times such as Christmas or Thanksgiving. I once was annoyed when I was asked to leave an exciting football game to remove a sewing needle that had become embedded in a buttock of a woman when she sat down on a chair. Needless to say, the game was over when I finished finding the "needle in the haystack." She was very patient, however, while I did the procedure under local anesthesia. Being called away during a period of fatigue is even more stressful. One early evening, Dr. John Clarke called me out to Waconia to see a patient with acute appendicitis. I remember my daughter, Jennifer, strongly urging me not to go because she knew I was tired. I did the appendectomy, but it caused something that could have been very disastrous. On the way home, I fell asleep and woke up in a shallow ditch after crossing a busy highway. I never told Jennifer about my near disaster.

Burdens

THE HEAVIEST BURDEN for all surgeons is telling relatives that multiple cancer metastases are found at the time of the operation. Also, there is sadness when informing a follow-up cancer patient (especially women) there is evidence of recurrence. Presentation of post-operative complications likewise is not pleasant. Sometimes all members of the medical profession in their careers have to meet these burdens. When a doctor chooses his career, he must realize that is part of the obligation.

Today, this burden is reduced by hospices, which shift the responsibility away from the individual doctors. These caring individuals deserve ultimate praise for their role regarding the nature of dying.

Reciprocity

ESPECIALLY DURING MY early surgical practice, there was an *esprit de corps* between doctors. Bedside or operating room assistance and consultation were frequently exchanged. Other surgical specialty doctors or family physicians, the latter with limited surgical privileges, might ask for help.

Gynecologists, for example may need assistance for intestinal surgery. On one occasion, I was requested to help when the colon was injured during an abdominal hysterectomy. A gynecologist asked me to check a patient's stomach for a tumor. After scrubbing up, I palpated the area and reassured him that it was not a tumor but only the pylorus of the stomach. In other circumstances, if a ureter was damaged during an abdominal hysterectomy, a urologist would be consulted.

One late afternoon I was about to leave for a meeting when I received a frantic call from a local dentist, asking me to come to his office immediately. While he was using a rotating disc, it skidded off the tooth onto the floor of the mouth, severing the left lingual artery. Even though he had put in a suture, bleeding continued under the mucosa, thus producing a large hematoma, which in turn produced marked airway compression. After I removed the patient's mucosal suture, blood was evacuated. The patient was then transferred to the operating room at North Memorial Hospital, where the lingual artery was ligated under local anesthesia. No charge was made.

Another time while a family doctor was repairing a right inguinal hernia, he also attempted to remove the appendix. In doing so, he inadvertently interrupted the blood supply of a portion of the small intestine, necessitating resection and bowel anastomosis. The patient did well, readily accepting his doctor's explanation. Again, I did not charge for the surgery.

On another occasion, I was interrupted from my home to help with a cholecystectomy. A cystic artery was continuing to bleed during the operation. Fortunately, the doctor had stopped the bleeding with a tamponade, thus avoiding damage to the common duct. I immediately enlarged the incision, removed the tamponade, and ligated the spurting artery. The following day, I had a serendipitous encounter with that doctor in which he displayed his ego and lack of humility. We happened to be changing dressings on respective patients who had adjacent beds. He called me over and introduced me to his patient upon whom I had prevented a hazardous complication. He mentioned nothing about my participation. I simply said, "Howdy," and then silently continued with my patient's dressing change.

Once, a call came from the operating room at Asbury Hospital requesting assistance on a patient who was undergoing an appendectomy. The surgeon, who had recently finished his surgical residency at the Mayo Clinic, wasn't able to find the appendix. Again, I immediately enlarged the incision, reflected the cecum, and removed the retrocecal appendix. He later referred a patient to Dr. Maxiener for a thyroidectomy. This harrowing experience of post-operative bleeding, requiring quick removal of the skin clips in order to prevent asphyxiation, induced him to quit doing surgery. He said that because he couldn't stand the stress of surgery, he was transferring his practice to Internal Medicine.

Sometimes help worked the other way. While in solo practice, prior to complicated elective surgical cases, I obtained the assistance of either Dr. Lyle Hay or Dr. Robert Utendorfer. I never used an assisting doctor without first receiving the patient's acknowledgement.

Atmosphere in the Operating Room

THE ATMOSPHERE IN the operating room is ordinarily serene; however, critical situations may interrupt that scene. The surgeon is the pivotal person. Sometimes surgeons have been known to throw instruments and in one rare case, a nurse received a laceration. If the operation is not proceeding smoothly, a doctor might place blame on the anesthetist or the surgical nurse. A retired nurse friend related a serious incident that occurred while she was a scrub nurse for a very pompous surgeon. Her right thumb was penetrated when an infected syringe was passed in the wrong direction. Massive infection required weeks of healing. The nuns who were in charge of the hospital in turn withdrew the doctor's surgical privileges. (Sharp instruments are always carefully passed with the blunt end first).

It might be the nurse who creates an uncomfortable atmosphere. One time at Mayo Clinic, I was invited to observe the brilliant surgeon Dr. Behrs, perform a right liver hepatectomy on my patient with a cancer of the right hepatic ductal system. Even though our conversation during the operation was amiable, I was uneasy because his overprotective nurse seemed irritated by my immediate presence.

I once asked my very good friend and Mayo-trained partner, Dr. Louis Buie what technique and demeanor the Mayo surgeons used in problematic situations. "One surgeon," he said, "would simply stop, quietly go over to the sterile water basin, wash off his gloves whether they needed it or not, gather himself and continue." One of the aforementioned physicians, Dr. Behrs, always kept calm by having music in the operating room, especially western music, his favorite.

To retain a calm atmosphere, I once told a shady joke, which produced some laughter. A portly woman consulted me for a cholecystectomy. During the initial visit, she asked if I had had any experience

with such surgery. A gregarious person, she had established a good ca-
maraderie with me during the pre-op examination and visits. While
scrubbing up, I looked over the operating room personnel in order to
see if there were any neophytes present. Not finding any, I then walked
over to the patient in order to answer her original question. I said, "I
don't know if I am capable of doing your surgery because last night I
put two books on my bedside table: one, *How to Do Cholecystectomies*
and the other, *One-hundred Ways to Have Sexual Intercourse.* I grabbed
the latter." And with that, her abdomen went up and down with laughter, accompanied by a similar chorus from the nurses. The abdomen
then resumed its normal position as the anesthesia prevailed. She later
kidded me about it. Although I always tried to maintain a comfortable
atmosphere, I sometimes regret that incident as being gauche.

In contrast, more serious dialogue can be effective. While I was
watching a very personal and talented Mayo Clinic surgeon do a cholecystectomy, he inadvertently cut the common duct. He hesitated then
looked up at the gallery of observing doctors and calmly said, "This
now is going to slow up my surgery schedule for the day." He then
added, "I guess I should have stayed in bed this morning." He proceeded in the same calm manner by deftly repairing the damage.

At another visit to the Mayo Clinic, I was anxious to observe a
famous surgeon who was noted for his expedient surgery. I waited in
the balcony for him to do an elective splenectomy. He was late because
his beloved noonday bridge game had delayed his arrival. Glancing up,
he noted I was the only observer. With that he proceeded, although
I had a hunch he was going to show off in front of the young yokel.
What happened next held me spellbound. When excessive bleeding
occurred, he became agitated. Even though I couldn't hear him, he was
castigating his assistant surgical resident. Multiple transfusions were
given, and finally the operation was over. This incident undoubtedly
was a unique event in the surgeon's very illustrious career. (Elective
splenectomy is relatively easy if the blood supply is initially dissected
out and ligated.)

I was reminded of one Dr. Maxiener's teachings: successful surgery depends upon the infinite care of the minutest details. Except for
his basso profundo voice going a few octaves deeper, he always kept
his cool. He once performed a cholecystectomy in which he severed

the common duct. Afterward, he walked into the doctor's lounge and dressing room and in front of a number of doctors announced, "After thirty years of surgical practice, I injured my first common duct." I admired his humility in admitting his error.

Hospital and Other Fees

PHYSICIANS, ASIDE FROM big disappointments in the care of some patients, may have mild disagreements in the doctor-to-doctor relationships. About forty years ago, when I was chief of staff at North Memorial Hospital, I became concerned about rising hospital costs. A suggestion was made to Vance DeMong, the hospital administrator, to post on each floor the cost of the most common charges; such as, daily room charges, various IV fluids, lab fees, dressing pack costs, daily oxygen and mistagan charges, along with periodic workshops to suggest simple measures to cut costs without detracting from excellent patient care. Another suggestion was to include a copy of a patient's bill in the discharge chart. Therefore, when the attending physician signed the discharge summary, he would be cognizant of the total hospital costs. I was informed that such specifics would be impossible. Not satisfied, I presented this at a monthly staff meeting, which went over almost with total silence. A chest surgeon accused me of going back to the medieval practice of medicine. I had no idea what he was talking about. The general attitude seemed to be, "What the hell, the insurance companies are paying the bill."

I made an attempt, nevertheless, to limit unnecessary charges. Of many examples, I have chosen three: 1) Rarely after surgery does a patient develop an unexplained rise in temperature. However, one time I was called back to the recovery room because my post-op patient's temperature had suddenly shot up to one-hundred and three degrees. The head recovery nurse asked, "Shall I order the cooling blanket?" "No, do you know what it cost just to have the blanket brought up here?" "No I don't." "To do so and hook it up for a few hours would cost at least seventy-five dollars; therefore, please put four ice bags on the patient and carefully monitor the rectal temperature. Call me afterwards if the temperature doesn't change. I will be back within an hour." While she was somewhat taken aback, she followed my orders. When I returned later, the temperature was normal, so the ice packs were removed. I learned this technique from Dr. Maxiener, who had used ice packs on patient's high fever during hyperthyroid crisis—thyroid storm.

2) Similarly, one Saturday when I was making "on-call rounds," I noticed one of our patients with mistagan—oxygen mask lying at the bedside, just "blowing in the wind." Knowing that it cost well over thirty-five dollars a day, I asked the patient if she felt the mask treatment was necessary. My partner Dr. Woyda advisedly had ordered the necessary therapy several days previously and unless the order was cancelled, twenty-four hour usage would have continued until discharge.

3) On another weekend on-call, I had a small confrontation with the daughters of a jaundiced eighty-year-old woman upon whom I had operated to remove her gallbladder and common duct stones. Desperately ill, she had been admitted via an ambulance. After her recovery, while I was standing near the nurses' desk, I informed the daughters that the mother was ready for discharge. "You'll call an ambulance then, won't you?" "No I won't." "Why won't you? She came by ambulance." "Yes, she did, but at that time, emergency hospitalization was needed, but not now. However, I will order an ambulance if you pay for it." In unison, they retorted, "It's free, Medicare pays for it." In return I said, "It's not free, you people, the nurses, and I pay for it." Not amused, they said, "How can we get her up the porch steps?" "Very simple, put your hundred-pound mother in a chair and each one grab a side of the chair and walk her up the stairs." (I had learned this technique from my father). The confrontation over, we went to the patient's room. I asked her if she thought she needed an ambulance to take her home. She easily got out of bed and said, "Absolutely not." Her daughters grudgingly accepted the defeat.

Cutting hospital costs are problematic because of patients' attitudes. Some people take advantage of the expensive ambulance service. It often happens with those on welfare who will, on occasion, call an ambulance to take their not-so-ill child to the emergency room. Hospital ambulance services are intimated because refusal could initiate ligation. At present, hospital bills are so ravaging high and complicated that any attempt to cut cost would be futile.

Once as secretary to the Minneapolis Surgical Society, I naively suggested having parity, along with a flexible standard deviation for common operations such as appendectomy and cholecystectomy. This statement evoked unanimous frowns. All of this took place before insurance companies proclaimed standard fees. While each doctor set his own fees, he sometimes conferred with others. When Dr. Lyle Hay and Dr. Robert Uttendorfer left the Veterans' Hospital for private practice, they asked others and me for average fee rates.

Trauma

BECAUSE OF NATIONWIDE metropolitan expansion, advancements in automobile technology and road improvement, car and crime injuries have risen. In the United States each year, over fifty thousand people are killed in car accidents. This figure is compounded by serious and minor injuries. To confront those emergencies, certain hospitals, which meet required standards, can be designated as trauma or burn centers. At the present time, except for organ transplantation, North Memorial is a total care hospital. However, at its incipiency, fifty years ago, the hospital was less sophisticated. North Memorial was strategically situated near new, busy Highway 100. The hospital received innumerable accident victims, especially after Vance DeMong, the administrator of the fledging hospital, innovated its own ambulance and helicopter service. As overall emergencies grew, the hospital needed expansion for space and emergency staffing. Except for the Minneapolis General Hospital, most of the private hospitals had no emergency room services. Initially, one other surgeon and I were the only staffed American Board General Surgeons at North Memorial Hospital; thus, I obtained much trauma experience.

Shortly after joining the staff of North Memorial Hospital, I was called to attend a twelve-year-old boy who had been hurt in an accident. His bicycle had been struck by a car and he was thrown thirty feet by the impact. The left leg was torn off just below the knee, along with the entire skin of the remaining stump. Dirt and grass were embedded in the muscle. Even though, surprisingly, he was not in shock, extensive debridement was necessary. Vance DeMong, the administrator, carried multiple bottles of irrigation saline to the operating room. Fortunately, since no infection set in, the healthy stump was covered with skin grafts. His injury was briefly mentioned in the newspaper, making him a bit spoiled by the shower of presents and money.

Multiple trauma cases increased as did the hospital and staff. These cases often required the cooperation of all specialties, such as orthopedic, urological, neurological, chest, plastic, and pulmonary.

Severe internal injuries may be devastating. One such patient was admitted to North Memorial Hospital after an accident with a big truck. His abdomen, which had been crushed against a loading platform, sustained a superior mesenteric artery injury, rupture of duodenum, and severe injury to the pancreas. Doctors Buie, Woyda and I decided after the superior mesenteric artery had been repaired, a Whipple procedure was required (A Whipple procedure requires a subtotal gastric resection along with the duodenum and the head of the pancreas; proper anastomosis is then needed to establish a gastrointestinal bowel and pancreatic drainage.) However, the patient developed multiple organ failure and expired.

A nurse's mother suffered a similar injury in a car accident. While the pancreas was not injured, the duodenum was completely transacted at the point where the pancreatic ducts entered the common bile duct. Even though initial duodenal repair was done, she developed recurring pancreatic drainage, causing further attempts at re-closure of the duodenum to fail. Hoping some more expertise surgery would prevail, I transferred her to the University of Minnesota. Every effort, however, was unsuccessful and she died. At that time, we did not have hyperalimintation. I am quite certain if we had, her life could have been saved.

At a different hospital, fifty-one years ago, Dr. Peggy Craig, a pediatrician, asked me to see a nine-year-old boy whose right arm had been run over as he was trying to cross the railroad tracks. One-half of his right forearm, along with the thumb, forefinger, and index finger was absent. There was also a minor injury of his left palm. Because the patient, Butch Bakken, was the same age as my son, I envisioned this as being my son.

I needed immediate consultation. Before the debridement, I consulted an orthopedic surgeon who advised amputation, stating there was danger of infections or "gas gangrene." I absolutely refused, commenting that we could always amputate if necessary, but not now. Extensive debridement was done, no infection developed, and later at an appropriate time, a plastic surgeon friend, Dr. Chesler, helped me skin graft the entire right side of his forearm. Butch loved sports, and after his arm was satisfactorily healed, the single mother was advised to "turn him loose"—play ball, hockey and other games. He eventually became a very low handicapper. At first Butch would hide his right arm behind his back, but later he would readily put out his right hand with the remaining little finger for a hardy handshake.

Several years later, while in a new Methodist Hospital, the same Dr. Peggy Craig asked me to see another young boy, who while riding his bike a in mall parking lot, had been hit by a car. He was stable even though he had a scalp laceration with a compression skull fracture, plus a compound fracture (bone exposed) of his left leg. A neurosurgeon, hesitantly because it was approaching dinnertime, finally responded. During the end of that surgery, the anesthesiologist informed me (as an interested spectator) that the patient's blood pressure had to be kept up with more intravenous fluid administration. In view of the forceful impact, I became suspicious that the cause of the fluctuating blood pressure might be due to an intra-abdominal injury. When the neurosurgeon was finished, abdominal exploration revealed rupture of the jejunum (small bowel at the ligament of Treits—junction of the duodenum and the small bowel). The ruptured bowel was sutured, the peritoneal cavity lavaged, and the abdomen closed. Then, an orthopedic surgeon was called and the compound fracture was treated. On rounds the next morning, I saw the boy sitting up in bed watching television. This was a classical situation, which, in multiple trauma cases, the literature advises that there should be a "captain of the ship." Fortunately, because of my experience with multiple traumas, I was able to assume that role.

Challenging Cases and Situations

During their careers, most doctors have major decisions and challenges. Questions arise. Should I call for a further consultation? Should I not make a midnight or early morning house or hospital call? Did I miss a serious diagnosis? Did I choose the wrong operative procedure? Am I shortchanging my family because of too much energy and time on medicine? The following anecdotal and challenging cases demonstrate the resolutions to those questions.

One such problem involved Dr. Byron McLaughlin, who at North Memorial Hospital tended a sixty-year-old patient with massive bleeding from his colon. The patient continued to bleed; and after admission of four units of blood, it was evident intervention was necessary. At surgery, the entire colon was full of blood. Since I did not know the bleeding site, I decided to resect the entire colon, following with an ilieo-rectal anastomosis. While the colon had multiple diverticula, no bleeding site was found by the pathologist. Recovery was uncomplicated. I accepted his three-hundred and fifty dollar insurance payment, and I refused his appeal to charge less. The Minnesota Medical Journal accepted my paper on "Bleeding as a complication of diverticulitis of the colon."

Another incident occurred with a Dr. Nash, also at North Memorial. He asked for consultation on a female patient who was in profound shock following the usual preparation for barium enema x-ray examination. She had an obstructing cancer of the lower descending colon. After proper administration of intravenous fluid and electrolyte, a transverse colostomy was done with an outpouring of a copious amount of a liquid fecal content. Within the next forty-eight hours, she became septic, along with abdominal pain and tenderness. These symptoms required immediate abdominal exploration. Surgery revealed an

140

entire necrotic colon down to the cancer site. After the entire colon was resected, low ilieo-sigmoid anastomosis was completed. She developed a clostridal bacterial septicemia (very toxic anaerobic bacteria).

Even though she surprisingly survived, a wound infection and poor nutrition resulted in an incisional hernia, which months later was easily repaired. If hyperalimintation had been available, the procedure would have been an ideal situation for this therapy. I accepted her very poor insurance coverage and continued to follow her until a few months before my retirement. Then, I willfully refused further care. I saw this patient every six months, each time doing breasts, abdominal, pelvic and proctoscopic examinations. In spite of all this work, her husband once challenged the thirty-five dollar office fee.

During the last visit, I clipped off a small low sigmoid polyp via the proctoscope, and for the next two or three days, she had a small amount of blood in her stool. I assured them there was no concern, but just to take it easy. About a week afterward, her husband called me and said she had lost three days of work and this was sufficient evidence for a malpractice suit. Following his threat, I wrote a letter terminating her care and assured her that her cancer was most likely cured. All of her records were available for referral. Twenty years later, she came to my wife's funeral and apologized for her husband's actions.

Another physician, Dr. Richard Williams, a very active and conscientious practitioner, called me to the emergency where an immediate decision had to be made. A young boy, after falling off his bicycle, was rapidly going into shock even though fluid administration was in place. He was rapidly transferred to surgery where exploration revealed the peritoneal cavity to be filled with undigested marshmallows. The impact of the bicycle handle had completely ruptured his stomach from the fundus (top) to the pylorus (bottom). He made a rapid recovery, but about one month later, required drainage of a small pelvic abscess. A small piece of marshmallow, which is an excellent culture medium, had apparently escaped the extensive peritoneal irrigation. Years later, the family asked me to attend his high school graduation.

Another time I was involved in an extremely precarious situation. At the Forest Lake Hospital, thirty miles north of Minneapolis, the only son of a very prominent Minneapolis contractor had been admitted in profound shock from a car accident. It began when the so-called compensation doctor called to say he was in a dilemma. He said the local doctor had called a St. Paul surgeon, but the family wanted me. "What should I do? Will you come?" "Okay," I said, "Call them back. I'll agree, but have the Sheriff's department meet us at the North Memorial parking lot. At the hospital I will pick up four units of type O blood—the universal donor blood."

We were rapidly escorted to Forest Lake where a very healthy appearing twenty-year-old male was in oligemic shock (blood loss). Nasal suction was implemented, blood rapidly administered via a cut-down and a urethral catheter inserted. After obtaining adequate blood pressure and urine output, the patient was transferred to the operating room. The peritoneal cavity was full of blood due to a splenic rupture. A splenectomy was performed with extreme difficulty because of the retroperitoneal left kidney hemorrhage, which had narrowed the peritoneal cavity into a clam-like space. At that point, when the patient's condition was stable, a left nephrectomy was mandatory.

With no trauma nephrectomy experience, I needed consultation. The patient was stable, so I went into an adjacent room, lit a cigarette and sought consultation. Calls to several urology friends were of no avail because they were in Chicago at an American College meeting. Another call was to Dr. Lyle Hay, who at that time, was in private practice and also teaching at Mount Sinai Hospital. I said to him, "Lyle, can you come out to Forest Lake? I have a stable patient who has a massive retro-peritoneal hematoma from a ruptured kidney." He said, "Go ahead, Doug, and take it out." He hung up. Knowing that the comp doctor's surgical ability was worthless, I was buoyed by Dr. Hay's confidence. I enthusiastically returned to the OR. The descending colon was quickly reflected, and the massive hematoma evacuated. In order to prevent uncontrollable bleeding, I squeezed and compressed arterial blood supply to the kidney with my left hand while clamps were applied to the arteries. The macerated kidney was then easily removed. After abdominal closure, the patient was returned to his room in stable condition. As a follow-up, I made daily rounds before and after transfer to Methodist Hospital.

Because of the overbearing compensation doctor, now long deceased, I met with the father of his only son in order to give complete probidity about his son's survival. I outlined from beginning to end with the role of each participating doctor. He had only one question:

"What do I owe you?" He gave me a check for eight hundred dollars and walked out of the office. Since I had just saved his only son's life, his attitude seemed callous and unappreciative. A few days later the comp doctor stopped me in the hospital and asked, "What did you charge?" "Eight hundred dollars," "Okay, I'll charge the same." In view of his minor role the comp doctor played in the surgical procedure, to me, his fee was excessive. So be it, to each his own.

Suicides

ONE CHALLENGING TRAUMA was so tragic that it has remained with me forever. My partner, Dr. Nemanich, removed a ruptured spleen from Neal Bechtol, an athletic eighteen-year-old boy, who was injured in a car accident in a near-by town. Following surgery, while in intensive care unit, he complained of an unusual amount of abdominal pain. He then went into shock. Being on call on this weekend, I was summoned. At surgery, his entire small bowel was black (necrotic), apparently due to injury of the superior mesentery artery, which supplies blood to the entire small bowel. My good friend Al Nash, the anesthesiologist, asked if abdominal closure was indicated. I chose to re-sect the entire small bowel and anastamosed the distal portion of his duodenum to a viable two inches of the terminal ileum. I needed to be careful during the anastomosis not to injury the ileal bowel mucosa. Intravenous hyperalimintation saved his life.

With such a minute amount of small bowel remaining, there was insufficient mucosal nutritional absorbing area to allow selective oral caloric intake. Furthermore, this lack of fluid absorption caused the dire complication of diarrhea. These after-affects produced catabolic complications, such as weight loss and interruption of normal neural hormones, which in turn, caused depression and psychotic behavior. Even though his life was miserable, he attempted college. After repeated episodes of futility, despondency and psychotic episodes, he committed suicide.

In retrospect, his subsequent suicide consumes me. Did I do the right thing? One answer might be: If I had answered Dr. Nash's question by not removing the foul smelling dead intestines, he would have had an unpleasant death within a few hours.

While most gun shot cases were taken to Minneapolis General

Hospital, I did have three episodes involving these dangerous weapons. A family physician and I were called from the Minneapolis Surgical Society Banquet to see a teenager who had tried to commit suicide. She had shot herself in the abdomen with a .22 rifle. The bullet had entered a loop of small bowel and the inferior vena cava. We began by suturing the bowel (two holes), then isolating the two holes in the vena cava by first placing tapes proximately and distally to the hole. The posterior wound was exposed by opening the anterior injury, thus allowing easy suturing. During recovery, I asked the young girl, "Why did you harm yourself this way?" She said, "I was angry at my father for reprimanding me about low high school grades."

In another attempted suicide, a retired executive became despondent because his driver's license had been taken away. He went out into his backyard, and shot himself in the left abdomen with a shotgun. The injury consisted of a splenic rupture and extensive damage to his colon and abdominal wall. That patient also survived without complications. Still another suicide attempt occurred when a man put the end of the shotgun barrel under his chin and pulled the trigger. When I saw him in the emergency room, only a portion of his skull was remaining. The emergency room nurse asked me what I was going to do. I simply covered the injury with dressings and allowed him to die within a few minutes.

More Unusual Cases, Some Successful, Others Not

ANOTHER CASE WAS indeed unusual. A young girl had fallen out of a tree and onto a tree branch, which penetrated the vagina and sigmoid colon without injury to her uterus. In this case, the patient also did well following the surgery for the stick removal and bowel repair.

Several of my trauma patients at North Memorial were not as fortunate. A young girl suffered severe liver rupture when she was struck by a car. At surgery, the hepatic veins, which entered the inferior vena cava, bled uncontrollably. She died on the table. Another case involved a retired minister who had suffered a chest injury and hip fracture after running off the road from too much imbibing. Before the operation, consultation was obtained from a chest surgeon, Dr. Frank Johnson. The hip fracture was pinned, but the patient succumbed later from pulmonary fat emboli. Another tragic car accident case involved a student who died from his injuries. He suffered severe head and abdominal organ injury plus a fractured tibia. He never regained consciousness. Adding to the tragedy, his mother had recently been widowed because of her husband's death in a fishing trip plane crash.

Shortly before retirement, there was one final challenge when I attended a patient who had been violently attacked. Dr. Mike Flannery, a talented emergency room doctor and also an avid and knowledgeable outdoorsman, paged me to see a stab victim, a young newlywed. Shock trousers, intravenous fluid, and oxygen were implemented on site by the paramedics. Prior to my arrival, Dr. Flannery had inserted a chest tube into a right hemothorax. Fourteen stab wounds were present on the abdomen and chest. A lacerated loop of small bowel was protruding out of a left abdominal stab wound. I quickly sutured the lacerated

146

bowel and then transferred the patient to the OR, where the entire chest and abdomen were prepped.

I quickly summoned my partner, the very able Dr. William Woyda, for assistance. At surgery, the abdomen was filled with blood. Exploration revealed blood coming from the left chest through a large laceration in the left diaphragm. Prior to this, the pericardial sac was aspirated of blood from the laceration in the pericardium. However, there was no heart injury. Utilizing a ring forceps, I pulled down the left lung lobe via the diaphragm laceration. A long lung laceration was quickly sutured. With the diaphragm sutured, the abdomen closed, I then opened the left chest. At that point, blood started to fill the tracheal tube. The problem was caused by a laceration between a bronchial branch and a pulmonary artery. This flow was quickly controlled with the removal of the lacerated lung suture. It was apparent that a left lower lobe resection was necessary. While waiting for a chest surgeon, I started dissection of the hilum of the left lung. Then a chest surgeon removed the left lower lobe, scrubbed out and headed for home. While we were closing the left chest, I noticed blood continuing to fill the right chest tube necessitating exploration of the right chest. When the surgeon returned from his home, we discovered that bleeding was coming from not only from several lung lacerations, but also from the main source, a laceration in the right internal-mammary artery. (This important artery runs parallel to the sternum and branches out into intercostal arteries, which course just beneath the ribs.)

The stoic young newlywed was discharged on her eighth post-operative day. Because of the dreadful experience, she required counseling because of the violence of the attack.

The circumstance of her injuries was very bizarre. A man had inquired about storage in the building that she owned with her husband. Since her husband was absent, she was showing the storage area when the young man suddenly began stabbing her. Severely wounded, she managed to call her sister who contacted 911. Medics, who performed emergency treatment at this site, initially saved the young girl's life. I appreciated Dr. Woyda's assistance as well as his compliment of my stewardship of the injuries.

Itinerate Surgery

THE AMERICAN COLLEGE of Surgeons has always been against itinerate surgery. A surgeon travels to other vicinities, performs the operations, and leaves the post-operative care to the local physicians. The basic reason for this is valid: The belief is that the original surgeon should stay with the patient through the entire care. While I agree with the College's principle that the post-operative care should be carried by the operative surgeon, other factors interplay.

At the time, itinerate surgery was widespread, not only in Minnesota, but elsewhere. Dr. Maxiener had practiced itinerate surgery for many years, receiving much praise from the referring physician and the hospital staff. I was never aware of his having any complications. The head of one surgical department of a prominent university would fly out and perform his specialty. The hospitals I attended were well staffed and sufficiently equipped except for certain facilities such as respiratory and intensive care units. Some were without qualified M.D. anesthesiologists. Furthermore, I never was aware of any iatrogenic infections. One factor plays a very important role: local residents prefer their own turf.

When I was in solo practice, I did itinerate surgery in order to meet expenses in the local fee splitting atmosphere. I was well acquainted with the referring doctor in my carefully selected cases. The exception, of course, would be emergencies. One of my main contributors was a hard working and conscientious young family practitioner, Dr. John Clarke. He worked in Waconia, Minnesota, a town thirty-five miles south of Minneapolis. As his practice grew in this community, he added associates, who also would send their referrals to me. Later, these local doctors were able to employ their own well-trained surgeon whose credentials they asked me to review. The new surgeon periodically asked me to perform surgery in cases where he felt inadequate. The hospital was able to obtain Dr. Kim as its anesthesiologist, who incidentally had expertise with acupuncture. In other areas, because of the growing population, most group partners obtained their specialists, especially in general and gynecological surgery.

I also went to Marshall, Minnesota, one hundred and fifty miles west of Minneapolis. I performed surgery for my fraternity brother, Dr. Kenneth Petersen, a family practitioner. Four other Marshall family doctors utilized me. Cases were carefully selected and set-up for a day of surgery. The doctors were not only referral physicians but they were also social partners. We would play music during surgery and on occasion combine a golf outing or steak dinner with the nurses.

Another place where I did itinerate surgery was at Madelia, Minnesota, about one hundred and thirty miles from Minneapolis. Dr. Bill Hruza, Dr. Harold Coulter, and a young associate were the only Madelia physicians. Dr. Hruza, another fraternity brother, did have three years of surgical training, but was uncomfortable doing surgery such as colon and gastric resections.

Regarding the cooperation of the local doctors and me, I refused to make financial deals. I told each doctor I would submit a fee, which would be reasonable. Realizing their time and help were valuable, I often reduced my fee, along with the qualification that if a patient complained, I should be notified. I never asked and I never knew what they charged. No complaint was ever received. I stopped doing itinerate surgery several years before retirement only because those places obtained their own competent doctors.

During those itinerate years, which mainly went well, I did have a few complications, for example, a patient bled from a gastro-intestinal anastomosis following a gastric resection. I was, however, in constant touch with Dr. John Eckdale, a Marshall physician. While the bleeding was not massive, it stopped, thus a return to the hospital was not necessary. Another time, an elderly man died at Waconia Hospital a day after a reparative surgery of a ruptured colon. The patient had an obstructing cancer of the sigmoid colon, which was ruptured after the patient had received castor oil in preparation for barium colon x-ray. At surgery, his abdomen was filled with massive amounts of feces and liquid fecal material that caused fatal septicemia.

Some challenging situations also arose at the Madelia Hospital. I was asked to consider the options for treating an eighty-year-old gentleman who had a fundic cancer of the stomach. At his bedside, I advised him that I preferred to do the operation in Minneapolis, where there was an excellent intensive care unit. He pointed his finger at me and retorted; "Listen here young fellow, I was born here and by God I am going to die here. I absolutely refuse to leave, and if I die, I won't hold it against you." Fortunately, he did very well and later moved into a nursing home where he assumed the leadership of the place. He sent me many holiday cards over the ensuring years.

One early morning, Dr. Hruza, one of the Madelia doctors, asked me to hurry out to perform a gastric resection for a massive peptic ulcer hemorrhage. Out of town, speed limits were broken. When I entered the patient's room, blood was splattered all over the walls. At that time, increased IV blood replacement was accomplished by squeezing a rubber ball attached to the transfusion bottle. The excessive pressure would force the excess flow into open space, hence all the splattered blood.

I asked to have the patient transferred to the operating room and said I would be there as soon as I had a quick bite and gulp of coffee. Just as I was putting on a scrub suit, a nurse rushed in and blurted out, "I think the patient died. As we were placing him on the operating table, the IV pulled out." When I entered, the nurse anesthetist was administering oxygen. I observed that the patient's pupils were okay and he appeared to be still alive. I said, "Keep the oxygen going."

Immediately cutting down to the saphenous vein through the unprepared skin and hair, I passed a plastic tube into his vena cava. While the nurse was pumping in fresh blood, the abdomen was rapidly opened through a midline incision. I lifted out the stomach and asked Dr. Hruza to hold it while I sliced it open. I then inserted a finger in the duodenum in order to compress the bleeding artery in the duodenal ulcer bed. Hoping to facilitate blood brain flow, with my right hand I compressed down on the weakly pulsating abdominal aorta. When the patient's blood pressure came up, his right hand and forearm pulled out of the restraint, and his hand came up over the incision. Then after the bleeding from the incision in the abdominal wall and stomach was controlled and the bleeding duodenal ulcer sutured, the nurses properly draped the patient. Glove changes were made, and then we did a gastric resection.

The next morning when a somewhat rested Dr. Hruza was making rounds, the patient commented, "You guys must have done a good job because I feel so much better." This hospital had an unusual advantage for such cases. A list of people who had a universal blood type was kept. Since these towns' people willfully donated blood during such emergencies, consequently fresh-drawn blood could be administered.

Another time during my itinerant practice, the phone rang while I was watching James Arness on "Gunsmoke." The caller asked, "Doug can you come out right away? We have a young girl who has been shot in the buttocks with a shotgun." I replied, "Can't you send her to the Mayo Clinic?" "No, it's too far away, and we don't want to move her." "Okay, I'll leave right away."

The Sheriff's department was notified that a doctor in a yellow Pontiac would be traveling over the speed limit on an emergency to Madelia, Minnesota. In spite, of the notification, just five miles from Waconia, I was pulled over by a deputy. He commanded; "Get out of the car. Lean over and spread your arms over the trunk." I tried to explain my speeding but he just ignored my pleas. I told him about the sheriff's verification, but for some reason he couldn't get through on his communication system. Finally, after reviewing my driver's license he believed me. Then after verification came through, I had an escort all the way through to Madelia.

On examination of the patient, I noticed the entry wound had occurred while she was bending over to attend the stove. The fifteen-year-old girl was babysitting the neighbor's infant. For some reason, the child's twelve-year-old brother shot her with a .410 shotgun at close range. The entrance wound contained shell wadding, but there were more seriously visceral injuries such as a shattered colon, small intestinal injury, loss of the left broad ligament, and destruction of the left fallopian tube and ovary. There was an extensive amount of feces scattered about the entire abdomen. After excessive lavages and small bowel repair, I did a right lower abdominal colostomy. Because of the anatomic relation of the left broad ligament, I was fearful that the ureter must also have been injured. Therefore, I found the proximal ureter and traced it to its transected end. While I had no experience of any type of ureteral anastomosis, I knew ureteral ligation would harm the kidney. To avoid this problem, I inserted a rubber catheter bringing it out of her left side as an ureterostomy.

By this time, it was dawn. When I reached Minneapolis, I ate a large breakfast of bacon, eggs, and hash brown potatoes at Hannah's Restaurant on Chicago Avenue. The breakfast cost thirty-five cents. After making hospital rounds, I went home to bed. Frequent follow-up phone calls revealed no complications. The highest post-operative temperature was ninety-nine degrees.

While the patient's family was poor, it was necessary to present a bill, even though I realized there would likely be no return payment. To my pleasant surprise, the townspeople, by holding benefits, paid the hospital expenses and my full-submitted bill of four hundred dollars. Drs. Hruza and Coulter received nothing. Years later, the girl went to the University of Minnesota, where she had the colostomy closed, along with the establishment of ureteral flow via small bowel segment anastomosis. Later, Dr. Hruza informed me she got married and was able to get pregnant. This entire experience proved that a family physician could successfully do long-term follow-up care.

In another case, this time at Marshall, Minnesota, Dr. Kenneth Petersen scheduled a female patient who had a cancer of the sigmoid colon. The tumor without liver metastases had become adherent to the uterus, the urinary bladder, a loop of the small bowel, and portion of the abdominal wall. At first, it appeared inoperable, except for a palliative colostomy. Fortunately, I was able to re-sect the sigmoid colon, the small segment of small bowel, a portion of the urinary bladder, the uterus, and a part of the abdominal wall. Then the bowels were anastamosed, the urinary bladder closed, and the operation completed. She made an uncomplicated recovery with no evidence of a recurrence during a long period of follow-up.

At least one time in my surgical, itinerate career, my advice proved beneficial. Before I ceased doing itinerate surgery, I was having a friendly discussion with an important board member of the American College of Surgeons. I admitted that I did selected itinerate surgery, frequently teaching some do's and don'ts. I told him while I was doing a case for a family practitioner, Dr. John Eckdale at Marshall, Minnesota, I advised him to have equipment to take care of sucking chest injuries. During one pheasant hunting season, Dr. Eckdale called me and thanked me for my prophetic advice. When a hunter had suffered a chest injury, Dr. Eckdale stabilized the patient with emergency chest care and then transferred him to another facility. As I remember, the American College of Surgeons board member appeared to be more amenable to the practice of itinerate surgery.

Friendships

ONE OF MY memories at this time in my career involved not only medical service but also friendship. After my residency, on my way to do surgery, either in Madela or Marshall, Minnesota, I always stopped at Green Isle in order to visit the Freudenthal Family. I became friends of Roy Freudenthal when he was a patient at the Veterans' Hospital. Roy, an entrepreneur, was outspoken, gregarious and jokeful. With his brother "Skelly", they owned an oil station. One day when I stopped at their oil station, Roy said, "I am having a lot of pain in my ass." "Let me take a look," I said. We went into an adjacent room that was filled with "For Sale" items, such as stoves, refrigerators and motley things. After finding an open area, I said, "Drop your pants so I can see the problem." Indeed, there was cause for pain. Peering out of his anus was a large thrombotic hemorrhoid. "Shall I fix it," I asked. "Sure, go ahead," he said. He bent over a desk and after injecting Novocain anesthesia I incised the hemorrhoid and evacuated a large thrombus (blood clot).

The delightful Freudenthal family was very close knit. Their mother Frieda was a fantastic cook who invariably supplied me with freshly baked succulent bread. Her husband, Fred was very jocular. Both Roy and Skelly emulated not only the father's sense of humor but also the warmth of their mother. Unfortunately, the mother developed breast cancer. After I performed a radical mastectomy, I was extremely dismayed because serous fluid persisted in accumulating under one skin flap. After I had performed repeated needle aspirations, the incision healed. Years later, when she died of natural causes, there was no evidence of cancer recurrence.

There was no sibling rivalry between the two sons, because Roy and Skelly, aside from being close business partners, had different in-

154

terests. Skelly loved to hunt pheasants and ducks and enjoy a few beers with his peers at the local pub. Years later when my son became of hunting age, Skelly would ask us to come out and hunt pheasants and ducks with him.

He also sought my service. He confided in me about his total sexual frustrations. His wife refused to have intercourse; however, they did have one child, a girl. Skelly, who delivered gas to the surrounding farms, told me during his deliveries he hesitantly refused many "obvious" housewives' invitations. Instead, he would leave and later, while in the truck relieve himself by masturbating. Less frustrating, perhaps was his gas delivery service. In order to replenish farmers' bulk tanks, he was on instant call. Usually most of the farmers wanted immediate refill at the time when "empty" appeared on the gauge. His offer to routinely maintain adequate fuel supply was not accepted. While not appreciating being called at unbelievable hours and even on Sundays and holidays, he was in essence a captive prisoner of his fuel truck. Miraculously, he escaped serious consequences when the station office explosion blew him out of the doorway.

His brother Roy was more successful in his endeavors with the opposite sex. When not engaged in bartering or making deals, he would go dancing. Even though he had a potbelly, he was surprisingly light on his feet. He would outclass Lawrence Welk in a polka or schottische contest. He rarely imbibed. In his late fifties, when he quieted down, he was caught in the marriage web, finally marrying his long-term, adoring girlfriend. I remained close friends with the family until one by one they passed on. These stops at Green Isle fill an important compartment of my memory.

Humor

WHILE MOST MEDICAL meetings are sedate, levity does unexpectedly occur. Once, during a University Saturday morning surgical review conference held in a large room filled with students and visiting doctors, Dr. Clarence Dennis, a youthful professor of surgery, was presenting the pinning of a hip fracture. With complete professional seriousness, he said, "Yesterday, we screwed this elderly woman." The auditorium rocked with laughter. Dennis' crimson face could be visualized from the high back rows. When my father first saw Dr. Dennis, he commented, "He looks like a damn kid."

One time at St. Mary's Hospital, Dr. John Toomey, a young and respected general surgeon, became frustrated during a paper presentation to a mixed meeting of doctors, nuns, and nurses. He said, "Before you do colon resections, you need to get rid of all orgasms." There were a few twitters, but after the second malapropism, there was silence, along with a prevailing sense of empathy. Dr. Toomey sadly died at a young age from rectal cancer.

At the Minneapolis general hospital conference, which I occasionally attended, I was present at a funny but sad moment. The highly regarded retired emeritus professor of internal medicine was allowed to retain his office long after his retirement. Even after he developed Alzheimer's syndrome, he was tolerated. He would give garbled talks and even accompany the staff on rounds. On one particular staff conference, he wandered down to the podium and in a loud voice said, "Gentlemen, this morning I woke up with an erection for the first time in a very long time." Out of respect, there was total silence. That apparently was his exit announcement.

Characters

ALL PHYSICIANS MEET interesting characters sometime during their careers. Of the many, I distinctly remember two patients especially. As a couple, they were definitely incompatible. I first saw the husband after he was admitted with hot coffee burns of his head, neck and shoulders. During an altercation, his wife had poured a pot of freshly brewed coffee over his head. Later during the holiday festivities, his wife, a beautiful, brown-eyed blond Swedish immigrant, was admitted to the hospital with third degree frostbite burns of her buttocks. While celebrating during a below zero night, she became inebriated, wandered out to a cornfield, sat down and fell asleep. Patches of buttock skin sloughed, but I allowed it to epithelialize, negating skin grafting. She told me that she wanted to leave him but didn't do so because she had very little education and no trade. After she was healed, I never saw them again, but pondered what was in the crystal ball for them.

Simple Advice

A T TIMES GASTRIC surgery may be avoided by simple communicative measures. An internist once called to inform me that he was referring a patient. Mr. Wolf, a prominent member of North Memorial Hospital's board of directors, was to see me for consideration for a gastric resection because of peptic ulcer bleeding. Being well acquainted with Mr. Wolf, I knew he was a very active businessman. In social conversations, I learned that aside from his avocation, his time was taken up with multiple board meetings. While he enjoyed his important position on the board, he was annoyed by all of the other expectations.

One day, while I was waiting for the elevator, Mr. Wolf greeted me. Pointing to a nearby hallway bench, I said, "Please sit down. If you have a few moments, I would like to talk to you about your problem. Your internist informed me that you wanted consultation about your bleeding ulcer." He acknowledged it, "Wolf," I said, "I am aware of your busy schedule, and I know that this is stressful." He agreed. I said, "Now, I do not advise surgery." I further suggested that he should immediately cease all stressful activities. Then I told him, "Retain your important position on the North Memorial Board and don't give up your two-a-day cigars and pre-dinner cocktail." Fortunately, after our friendly conversation, he had no more peptic ulcer complications.

Adverse Medical Judgment

DURING MEDICAL CAREERS, all doctors encounter situations of discrepancies in judgment. I recall four incidents where this occurred. One case of acute appendicitis taught me to be less opinionated and more appreciative of the family doctor's expertise. Dr. Greg Schissell, a long time friend and family doctor, called and asked me to see a female patient with acute appendicitis. After my examination, I advised antibiotic therapy for what I diagnosed as pelvic inflammatory disease. Dr. Schissell initially accepted my decision. However, after a few hours of conservative therapy, he called, emphatically insisting that she should have surgery, either by me or by someone else. The emphatic gesture prompted me into action. At surgery, she had suppurative appendicitis (appendix gorged with pus). The appendix was positioned adjacent to the uterus and broad ligament, therefore mimicking pelvic inflammatory disease. Not only did he accept my apologies but also my praise for his diagnostic acumen.

The second case demonstrated a disparity in diagnosis in which I performed and explored something not necessary. I saw a thirty-year-old female whose physical signs were pathognomonic of pelvic inflammatory disease. The referring family doctor became irate, practically demanding surgery for appendicitis. I acquiesced and, to prove a point, I made a small muscle-splitting incision in the right abdominal lower quadrant. After incising the peritoneum, I observed milky peritoneal fluid spilling into the incision, confirming my diagnosis. I was able to tease up and visualize a healthy appendix. I did not feel triumphant, only abashed that I had been trapped to do an unnecessary operation.

While the following third case didn't trap me, the doctor's demands were disconcerting. During one bitter winter midnight, soft-spoken Dr. Fred Wolter awakened me, requesting my presence in the emergency room of North Memorial Hospital. Softly but emphatically he said, "I have my dentist friend, with whom I share office space, now in the emergency room. He has a known peptic ulcer with upper quadrant abdominal pain."

Not being overly anxious to endure a fifty-mile round trip, I began with some questions. "Does the upright abdominal x-ray show free air under the diaphragm? Does he have any breathing shoulder strap pain? Is the white count normal? Is there evidence of rebound abdominal tenderness?" (Found with peritoneal contamination). His answer, "All negative." "Oh," I said, "Insert nasal suction, administer a mild narcotic, and call me if doesn't show improvement. He has a penetrating duodenal ulcer, not a perforation." "No," he insisted, "You come or I will call someone else." So I said, "I'm on my way." I went from under the warm covers to the cold car and sped to the hospital. After I instigated conservative therapy, the patient rapidly responded. Because of fatigue, I didn't dictate a consultation. Furthermore, I didn't submit a bill because the patient was Dr. Wolter's close friend and a fellow health provider.

My final case was through an encounter with Dr. Wolter but had nothing to do with interacting judgment. In a tragic fire that engulfed his home, his child suffered severe body burns. Although he asked me to treat her, without hesitation, I transferred the responsibility to the able pediatric surgeon, Dr. Tague Chisholm. I had always disliked caring for extensive body burns, especially in children.

One child's care at Fairview Hospital, however, was enjoyable, a contrast to the previous four cases. A young boy had second-degree burns of his legs and third degree burns of his buttocks. In most severe burn cases, the patients lose their appetite; therefore, maintaining adequate nutrition is vital. To induce the boy to eat and drink the high caloric supplement, I bribed him with money. If he would eat and drink the required amount, he was promised a daily allotment of twenty-five cents. He made certain he received each daily allotment. By maintaining his nutrition, he responded well. After many hospital days, he returned to his farm home where several buttock-granulating patches were left to epithealize. Even though he suffered a great deal of pain, he accepted his injury and treatment willingly. Each hospital visit for me was fulfilling.

Shared Experiences with Dr. Clarke

A FURTHER AND MOST memorable occasion involved Dr. John Clarke, who at that time, administered hospital cares in a converted large residence. With his familiar Texas drawl, he said, "Doug, I have a two-year-old child out here who has an acute appendix." My answer, "Two year-olds don't get appendicitis." He contested, "That may be true but this one <u>does</u> have appendicitis." I drove thirty miles to Watertown, Minnesota, and in that old hospital under ether anesthesia, we removed a badly infected appendix. Over the next twenty-five years, I continued to be aware of John's diagnostic acumen. I don't remember the eldest patient I had operated upon for appendicitis, but John Clarke's appendectomy case was the youngest.

At that same hospital, I didn't perform major gastrointestinal surgery, but I did several herniophories and even a radical mastectomy. From the latter operation, I once saved a lady's life as remembered by Dr. Clarke. He said she lived many years afterwards, finally succumbing from natural causes.

Dr. Clarke and I didn't just associate at the operating table but the kitchen table as well Whenever we did surgery, part of the agenda involved eating. The highlight of the visits took place in the old kitchen. The hospital cook was a large German lady who completely and naturally fulfilled that role. The enticing aroma of baking consumed our nostrils, even though we had on masks. After post-operative duties were performed, we went directly to the kitchen. There, we devoured generous pieces of fresh apple pie topped with slices of cheese, all washed down with fragrant coffee. She would always stand sidewise by the stove with a watchful gaze out of the corner of her eye. On the way out, I would stop to hug her and shower her with honest praise for her culinary ability. While she didn't smile or say much, her eyes bestowed appreciation. Dr. Clarke once told me how much she enjoyed our tête-à-tête, and if I wanted to insult her, it would be not to visit the kitchen. He added, "Don't you ever leave without stopping. I don't care how much of a hurry you are in." The captivating cook's name, according to Dr. Clarke's dictionary memory, was Frieda Bandemyer.

During those years of association, Dr. Clarke and his wife Lynn became close friends with my wife and me. After opera attendance, we would meet in our country home, where Eudora and Lynn would sing duets. Operatic arias would be played while we ate Eudora's gourmet food. Tragically, Lynn passed away in April 2005, from metastatic breast cancer.

Fee Splitting

F EE SPLITTING WAS a significant ethical consideration. During my surgical career, I had three instances of fee differences between doctors. The first case involved Dr. Al Wolf. While making rounds at Asbury Hospital, Mrs. Whaley, the second floor nurse, called me to the phone and said, "Dr. Al Wolf wants to talk to you." He then said, "Doug, drop your fee on that last appendectomy because when we did surgery on that elderly woman with gall stones and common duct exploration, I didn't receive anything. I will send the bill in for the appendectomy." I said, "Al, I don't work that way. I received one hundred and twenty-four dollars for that cholecystectomy and common duct exploration and I am satisfied with that remuneration. I'm more satisfied that we saved the jaundiced woman's life." Bang went the phone after he retorted, "I'll get somebody who will negotiate." Indeed, he did. He found a former fraternity brother of mine who had some surgical training. Ironically, previous to that conversation, I had operated on his office nurse for an ectopic pregnancy. I did not send a bill.

Also, I had earlier congratulated him for his family practice altruism as he left to make rounds at a few nursing homes. During that time, we were receiving minimal old-age benefits. He said he would make over a hundred dollars that day simply by following what the payment code allows. That incident polarized my negative opinion of him. Shortly thereafter, he moved to Florida and our paths never crossed again.

The second incident occurred as a referring family physician and I were scrubbing up for an appendectomy. I was consulted because his associate's referring surgeon was unavailable. He commented that surgeons charged too much, thus insinuating that the referring doctor didn't get enough. I was bewildered by that comment because I was cognizant that their consulting surgeon made them "deals." I retorted,

"That is not the problem. You referring and assisting family doctors charge too much for what you don't do and not enough for what you do." There was no response.

Another disruptive incident took place in a busy corridor of North Memorial Hospital. An extremely intelligent family doctor, who was on self-management for his bipolar personality, suddenly stopped me. In a noticeably loud, accusing voice said, "Your fees are too high and my assistance fee is too low." I immediately rebuked him by telling him, "Fine then, don't call me. It will be very easy for you to find another surgeon who will conform to your demands." Nothing more was said and we still stayed friends. I continued to work amiably with him.

The next unpleasant episode with a doctor was not about fees, but it did have a primary undertone. There was an element of referral antics. Our conversation took place during a cocktail hour at a hospital golf outing. A gynecologist friend openly asked me if I would do a favor for him. He said, "Doug, I know that you do surgery at Waconia Hospital. Would you put in a good word for me, in order for me to do their GYN surgery?" My response was immediate, "You want me to do that for you, knowing that all your GYN surgery referrals go to another surgeon." His answer: "Doug, yes, I must do so because he has something on me." That ended that conversation.

Adverse Power

During the forties, hospital committees were not very strict. An excellent and much admired surgeon, Dr. Roscoe Webb, made futile attempts to have hospitals require verification of a doctor's proper training before allowing him surgical privileges. Now, all accredited hospitals have rigid qualifications, controlled by the watchful eyes of the anesthesiologists, pathologists, and surgical committees.

In the thirties and early forties, a doctor could apply for membership in the American College of Surgeons if he were recommended by a local college member. While an initiate could do some surgery, he would usually refer major cases to the recommending surgeon. I regarded that as entering via the "backdoor." At present, the College has very strict qualifications for membership. Not all of the seven private Minneapolis hospitals at that time had full time administrators or pathologists.

During my productive years, racial intolerance was prevalent. Jewish MD's had a very difficult time being accepted into hospital staffs. I met a young well-trained surgeon who repeatedly had been refused hospital membership. Disgusted and disheartened, he moved to California. Because of the frustration in the Jewish community, a fund raising dinner was held in which money was pledged towards Minneapolis Mt. Sinai Hospital. There, one's heritage was not an issue for staff admission.

In the forties and earlier, some doctors were self-appointed prima donnas. No one crossed their paths; if so, careers were in jeopardy. A victim of these powerful doctors was Dr. Stuarman, my father's country doctor friend. He left a busy family practice in Erskine, Minnesota, in order to receive a pathologist degree under Dr. E.T. Bell at the University of Minnesota. Following that appointment, he accepted a pathology position at a prominent Minneapolis Hospital. He accurately reported gross and microscopic findings of all surgical specimens. If an appendix showed no microscopic infection, his report was: "appendix with no infection." If the gallbladder contained no stones and no evidence of inflammation, he would report: "gallbladder with no infection." Those honest reports inflamed some of the surgeons, and Dr. Stuarman was fired as being incompetent. He was too honest. He then moved to California where he opened his own laboratory. Although the prima-donnas gradually faded away, there was one skilled surgeon who defied attempts to censure him. A few examples will illustrate his power. During one operation following a colon resection, a sponge was inadvertently left in an elderly lady. In spite of recurring problems, the doctor refused to operate. The symptoms were ignored and the patient died.

In another incident, a patient after a cholecystectomy consulted a doctor for upper abdominal distress. X-rays revealed an upper intra-abdominal sponge, and thus the patient was referred to the initial surgeon. His pre-operative diagnosis was an incisional hernia. He covered up his mistake by surreptitiously removing the sponge. Believing the ruse, the patient later went back and told the other doctor that his abdominal distress was caused by an incisional hernia.

Several other cases involved errors that patients would never know. A middle-aged man died from bile peritonitis following a cholecystectomy. The surgeon turned all of post-operative care over to the referring internist who took the blame. Another patient expired from post-operative tetany following a thyroidectomy. The error was shifted to the referring family physician for failure to do adequate follow-up. (Low calcium produces tetany and occurs after parathyroid insufficiency. The four parathyroid glands regulate calcium blood levels). A boy died from septicemia following a splenectomy for a calcified splenic mass. Post-operative care was shifted to another surgeon, who again, took the false accusation.

In the mid-forties, questions were raised regarding the all-too-common practice of removing appendices. Several articles appeared at that time relative to the accepted percentage of normal appendices. My reviewing of one hundred cases of appendectomies done at the old Minneapolis Asbury Hospital found that forty percent of the appendices were microscopically normal. Utilizing the history, physical and laboratory reports, along with giving the operator the benefit of the doubt, I came up with a statistical fourteen percent of the normal appendices that were still selected for operation. I was to present my findings at the monthly staff meeting but was bumped by the chief of staff for another talk. Later, I was able to give the results at a hospital surgical conference. Dr. Sam Nerenberg, a highly intelligent and industrious pathologist, confirmed my research by later informing me that the percentage of normal appendices fell to about twenty percent, subsequent to my presentation.

At one time, religion caused a humorous, but tragic interruption of hospital routine. Religion was occasionally influential in everyday hospital atmosphere. One day, while making rounds at St. Mary's Hospital, I was suddenly cognizant of an unusual commotion in the corridor. The nuns, priests and rabbis, along with some Jewish families, were shouting and scurrying about in this otherwise quiet and serene atmosphere. I asked the nun at the information desk what precipitated this uproar.

A high-ranking rabbi had traveled to Minneapolis in order to perform a religious circumcision on a newborn of a prominent Jewish family. When the baby's penis was exposed, the penis had already been circumcised. Since interns were paid only twenty-five dollars a month, it was custom to have all the baby boys circumcised so the intern could receive a little extra money, in this case, the usual five dollars. Everything cooled down when the rabbi apparently took another little snip.

I recall only two other errors, one of which might have had a dire effect. Dr. Maxiener used a syringe to aspirate purulent urine from the right kidney via a ureteral catheter. He requested the attending nurse to inject dye into the intravenous tubing, and then asked for a syringe to repeat aspiration. (It was the same syringe with its residual dye puerile content). At first, there was near panic, expecting septicemia. As an observer, I was scared. As the surgeon, Dr. Maxiener was distraught. The nurse stood by petrified. Pus injected into the bloodstream can be lethal. The female patient luckily had absolutely no complication.

Another case occurred in a patient who was supposed to be having nasal suction. Prior to wall suction, nasal tubes were connected to a bottle system in which negative pressure was created in one bottle by gradually emptying another large bottle. Inadvertently, the nurse had reversed the tubes; the patient's nasal tube, instead of having suction was receiving fluid. When I entered the patient's room, he complained of fullness. About twelve-hundred to fifteen-hundred cc's of water had been given. No complication occurred, however. Because everyone, including doctors, are all human, mistakes are inevitable, some humorous, some sad and tragic, some reversible and some not. Many are forgotten, others forever haunt the practitioner.

Avarice

IN GENERAL, THE medical profession is a noble one. Over the years from 1942 until retirement in 1982, however, I was aware of some tarnishing things. Prior to the early forties, ophthalmologists would receive kickbacks from referrals to optical companies. A few doctors who did compensation work for companies would ask the injured person to make repeated "necessary" office calls. One doctor showed me a film of a fractured arm. Even though the film had been read and charged by the attending hospital radiologist, he charged the insurance company for his personal review. "That way," he said, "I can get more compensation for the fracture."

Another physician belonged to a luxurious club at a notable Minneapolis downtown men's club. It was a way to rub elbows with CEOs of large companies, so he could lobby for their compensation work. He personally related to me that long and detailed dictated descriptions of a simple laceration could entail a higher return.

Sometimes, internists, after referring a healthy patient to a surgeon, would stop by every post-operative day, say hello, take a blood pressure, and later submit daily hospital bills. To say hello is fine, but to charge is not.

Of all the shortcomings in medicine, avarice was one of the most prevalent. Once a laboratory technician who was a friend of my wife quit her position in a small Minneapolis hospital because of her dismay about the large discrepancy between normal surgical and a pathological tissue finding. She was especially concerned about the huge number of normal uteruses that had been brought to the pathology laboratory. The major contributor was a charismatic Scandinavian family practitioner, who, at age fifty, stated he was going to retire with one million dollars. His proclamation fulfilled, he moved to California with his bank account of one million. That extra money from the questionable lab reports didn't prolong his life, however, since he died at age sixty. The small hospital closed several years after he left, presumably because of the loss of his admissions.

Hernia operations can lead to the abuse of over-charging. Infants, especially males, because of the descending of the testicles into the scrotum, may develop a bilateral inguinal hernia. I asked a surgical colleague if he always explored the opposite side after the obvious one. He said he did, always finding a hernia (peritoneal bulge)on the other side, which allowed him to bill for bilateral hernia repair. Personally, I always explored the other side via a one-centimeter incision. If no hernia was found, I either negated the charge or submitted a very minimum fee.

Unearned charges sometimes are submitted following "ghost surgery," wherein the patient's doctor would submit a total surgical fee even though he was only an assistant. The person who performed the operation would then be paid by the patient's original doctor. A prime example of unearned fees often took place within the anesthesia department of North Memorial Hospital. Once, Dr. Dunlap, a very prominent urologist, and I caused quite a stir in the North Memorial MD anesthesiology department. Unless it was a spinal or upper extremity nerve block, the nurse anesthetist would administer the anesthesia during the operation. The MD would be there during the induction, and in most cases, at the end. If an MD were needed during the operation, he would be called from the lounge, frequently, interrupting the doctor's nap, chess game or TV program.

It was not unusual to have three rooms running. One MD stayed on until the full schedule was completed. Anesthesiology fees were based on the length of the surgery. In other words, if three rooms were running, each patient would be charged for full time. Of course, all the other patients were charged for full time coverage, even though the nurse anesthetist who administered the anesthesia was there full time. The hospital bill also included the nurse anesthetist fee in the surgery room bill. We brought this unnecessary practice to the administrator's attention; therefore, we weren't very popular. Eventually, however, changes took place, wherein the hospital would bill separately for the anesthetist, and the anesthesiologist would bill for their expertise and personal time.

Even more avaricious is the mortician profession. Undertakers universally have a reputation for excessive charging. Their fees have always disturbed me. Dr. Maxiener used to say, "Present the bill when the tear is on the cheek." After my wife's father died, Eudora and her mother asked me to choose a casket. I went to the funeral parlor where the owner, Mr. Erickson, sickeningly patronized me. "Doug, how are you?" "Show me the choices," I said. "You'll especially like this one," he said. "Yes, I know, but Eudora told me about a less expensive one." "Oh yes that one," he reluctantly said. "We'll take it. You know, Phil didn't leave very much. Phil doesn't need it and Lilly does," we countered. With that decision, his attitude completely reversed to tolerant conversation.

On one other occasion, I happened to be standing nearby when my cousin Eldith Adkins was leaving the funeral home with the undertaker at her side. In a relatively loud voice, I asked her what the bill was. Answer, "Six thousand dollars." They both heard my reply, "If I had charged one-third or one half that amount for a life saved by surgery, I would have been called a crook." It was not an appropriate thing for me to say.

The following cases represent a subtle method of cupidity or just poor judgment. When laparoscopic technique was innovated, I became interested in its usage, especially utilized by gynecologists. Its value lies in the diagnosing the etiology of the enigmas of chronic lower abdominal pain where the history and pelvic examination were not diagnostic. I reviewed all such cases at North Memorial Hospital in order to determine its value. Of these, a statistical significant number were negative. Only two positive cases of endometriosis (a painful condition caused by uterine endometrium proliferation on the peritoneum outside the uterus) were found. Of significance, however, is that the negative majority was done by one gynecologist and primarily on welfare women.

The following case definitely represents poor judgment with a possible pecuniary element. When my wife's violin teacher, Arnold Arnson, a highly skilled but financially poor violinist, developed advanced stomach cancer, I referred him to the indigent care service under the supervision of Professor Dr. Lyle Hay at Mount Sinai Hospital. Physical examination revealed formation of peritoneal metastases as evidence of a *rectal shelf* (abdominal metastatic tumor cells accumulating in a mass in a cul-de-sac above the rectum). This finding was a contraindication for surgery, and Dr. Hay so informed Arnold's sister who was her brother's financial support. Not convinced, she consulted her internist who, in turn, referred Arnold to his son-in-law surgeon. After surgery, which consisted of an *open and close* of the abdomen, Arnold developed distressing massive abdominal ascites (accumulation of serous fluid). Since the surgeon refused house call requests, as a friend, I periodically went to his sister's home to aspirate the fluid. He courageously accepted death.

When I was in solo practice, no charge was submitted to doctors' families, nurses, ministers, priests or nuns. Insurance payment was acceptable. One incident revealed an attorney's attempt to take advantage of this principle. I treated a retired minister, but he subsequently died. After filling out several insurance forms, I submitted a two-hundred dollar fee. I shortly received a return letter from the daughter, who had apparently been informed of my edict that I didn't charge ministers. Knowing that the family had insurance coverage, I wrote back and said if the attorney and the undertaker would reduce their fees, I would reduce mine at the same percentage. A check for two-hundred dollars was received from the attorney with no attached comment.

Malpractice

MALPRACTICE IS A "Sword of Damocles" over the head of all doctors. The extremely high cost of malpractice insurance has caused some obstetricians, for instance, to cease delivering babies, especially in high-risk cases. On a personal level, I was once threatened by a post-thyroidectomy patient because of alleged laryngeal nerve damage He blamed me for his hoarseness. I sent him to an Otolaryngologist, who diagnosed chronic laryngitis caused by heavy smoking. Since the vocal chords had normal function, the case was dropped.

In another case, I was fearful of being sued. A sump suction drain was inserted after a cholecystectomy. The next day suction was disconnected, the plastic drainage tube shortened, and a safety pin inserted in order to hold the drain above the exit wound. At the next morning dressing change, no drain was visible. The patient said that during the night when he turned over, he felt something different happening. Since x-rays in the operating room showed no displacement of the drain, it was easily removed. While the patient was satisfied with my explanation, his son, who happened to be an attorney, was a bit accusatory and threatening. Nothing more happened.

Serious errors can occur, simply because of inadequate or inappropriate communication. After I finished my residency and on my first day of partnership with Dr. Maxiener, I became aware, that he had made a serious surgical error. This was caused by miscommunication. On that day, I was cognizant of unusual commotion coming from the examining room. Several shrill voices overwhelmed Dr. Maxiener's voice, which usually rebounded above all others. This time, however, I noticed his voice was subdued. It was obvious the discussion was not jovial. To find out the cause of this uproar, I asked Ardis Halquist, our office nurse to come into my office. Aghast, she then related this scenario.

Dr. Moses Barren, the most prominent Jewish internist, had referred a woman to Dr. Maxiener for consideration of a breast biopsy. Dr. Maxiener, who had suffered hearing loss during his artillery service in World War I, apparently misunderstood Dr. Barren's consultation. Instead of performing a biopsy, Dr. Maxiener did a simple mastectomy. Following the operation, he met with the husband and relatives, informing them the mastectomy went smoothly. In unison, they said, "She must have had cancer; otherwise, you would have not performed a mastectomy!" Undoubtedly, Dr. Maxiener must have been speechless. It so happened that the Mount Sinai pathologist was also a Barren and a close relative of Dr. Moses. The breast was carefully scrutinized and after several microscopic sections, evidence was found that was suggestive of "pre-cancerous cells." Multiple meetings with the patient, the relatives and Drs. Barren and Maxiener satisfied the family, thus preventing malpractice litigation.

An incident involving me at the old Asbury hospital may have seemed to some as unprofessional. While I was making rounds, Mrs. Whaley, the second floor head nurse asked me to examine a female patient who was in post-operative shock. Her blood pressure was unobtainable. While her doctor, who had performed a cholecystectomy, was on the way, I immediately took direct action. Blood was pumped in via a venous cut-down. The attending doctor later appeared, at which time her blood pressure was adequate. He held her hands and softly commented to me, "Her blood pressure is normal." "Yes," I said, "After multiple blood transfusions, a blood pressure of one hundred and twenty is a lot better than lethal levels when I first saw her." Operative intervention was obviously needed. Even though I was willing and anxious to assist, he summoned his family practitioner friend to assist in re-exploration, following which the patient expired. At a later surgical conference, he mentioned only something about an abnormal blood supply to the gallbladder. I was convinced that her life would have been saved if re-exploration had been performed by qualified and better-trained surgeons who would be well aware of biliary anatomical abnormalities.

At another time, I was guilty of interference. In this case, the same two family physicians explored a jaundiced lady. After cancer was found in the head of the pancreas, the abdomen was closed. The family requested consultation. She was dehydrated, had electrolyte imbalance, and was exhausted from scratching the deepening jaundiced skin. I agreed to take over the case only if her doctor was released and if a trained surgical assistant could assist me. After the husband agreed, I quickly administered intravenous electrolyte replacement. The next day we operated and confirmed the diagnosis. In addition, we did a bile duct bypass in order to establish bile drainage with resolution of the intractable itching. While the patient and husband were grateful, the irate doctor threatened, but never did report me to the Hennepin Medical Society. Some of my peers felt that it was inappropriate of me to have interfered, even though it relieved her itching. Nine months later, she died.

Medical Ethics

MEDICAL ETHICS HAVE remained the same with the following exceptions: advertising and acceptance of sterilization procedures (tubal ligations and vasectomies) and abortions. In the early fifties, for example, I scheduled a right inguinal hernia on a forty-four year-old female. Just before surgery, she asked me if I could ligate her fallopian tubes at the same time. I dictated the operation as a right hernia repair and bilateral tubal ligation. The chief of surgery, who happened to be a gynecologist, called me on the carpet and warned me never to do that again. I had neglected to follow the proper sterilization protocol. I told him that she already had raised a family. If she got pregnant and had a vaginal birth, it would certainly break down the previous surgical vaginal perineal repair. His answer, "Another surgical repair could always be done." I was left speechless.

Mysteries About Cancer

EVERYONE HOPES THAT some day all of the mysteries of malignancies will be solved. During my career, I became aware of its vagaries. Variable prognostications can be made by the type of the cancer under the microscope. Also, sites and dimensions of the specific organ location, evidence of local invasion and/or metastases, duration of symptoms, prior to the diagnosis and treatment, are important prognostic factors. For instance, over ninety percent of patients die within eleven months after the first symptom of pancreatic cancer. Several anecdotal cases will exemplify its treachery as well as its forgiveness.

Overwhelming results may occur both with favorable or unfavorable prognostic elements. One such case is that of a young male adult who died from metastases two years after I had resected the descending colon for a relatively small cancer. This result was the opposite of another patient of Dr. Kenneth Petersen's in which long term survival occurred. She lived even though the sigmoid colon cancer had multiple adjacent organ and abdominal wall invasions.

Another example of this mysterious phenomenon is illustrated in the case of a young divorced mother of two teenagers. I performed a mastectomy on her left breast for a small cancer in the upper and outer quadrant. The size, location and especially negative axillary lymph nodes prognosticated a favorable eighty-five percent or more five-year survival. However, two years later, bone metastases crept in (She had remembered me from her St. Mary's proby nursing days). I admonished her but admired her courageous and devoted behavior. I was critical because she was cognizant of the mammogram findings several months before seeking treatment. She accepted my admiration for her response to her personal tragedy.

Two cases of lingual (tongue) cancer illustrates the killer's manifestations. I referred Dr. Roger Anderson's wife, Agnes (a non-tobacco user) to the Mayo Clinic for surgery of a small cancer on the side of her tongue. Just months after surgery, she developed massive neck lymph node metastases, and she died a horrible death.

Another tongue cancer with extreme characteristics was exhibited in a patient who had a profound addiction to nicotine. The cancer of the back of his tongue was so large that my visualization was impaired. It was so massive he was unable to fully open his mouth. A "commando" operation described by Drs. Varco and Dennis was performed. This consisted of exposure of the tumor by making a vertical incision through the midline of the lower lip down to the mandible, which was then transected and spread in order to obtain a surgical approach. This exposure allowed extensive tongue resection along with the lower pharynx wall and a portion of the floor of the mouth. The operation was finished with a "pull through" radical neck dissection for removal of draining cervical lymph nodes. As I remember, the nodes contained no metastases. During the next morning rounds, I found him calmly sitting up in bed attempting to smoke a cigarette. After his surgery recovery, his sister took him to the University Cancer Clinic for a long-term follow-up. The University physicians were astounded that this procedure had been done by a surgeon outside of their realm. While I received no compensation, I was amply awarded by self-satisfaction.

Malignant melanomas may defeat prognostication protocol by erratic behavior. Microscopic depth of the skin lesions is a very important factor as well as evidence of lymph node spread. Size and location of the lesion may be of value. Malignant melanomas may occur in any organ where melanoma cells are present, such as in the skin, retina, and even in the gastro-intestinal tract. During my years of private practice, I recall four cases in which some of these elements were demonstrated. In one incident, a teenage girl died from metastases about two years after a big toe amputation. She had a malignant melanoma located beneath her big toenail. Another case involved a beautiful young newlywed. The malignant melanoma on her calf was treated with excision and a skin graft. Long-term follow-up of ten or more years showed no evidence of recurrence. In the case of a middle-aged man, a partial ear lobe resection of a small malignant melanoma was performed. The operation resulted in a long-term remission.

A fourth case reveals vagaries which amaze me even now. In 1957, a healthy Norwegian who was an expert cabinetmaker underwent wide resection and skin grafting for a malignant melanoma on his back. Several years later, another malignant melanoma was similarly treated. He later developed extensive right axillary lymph node metastases. The black tumor-filled nodes were removed by axillary node dissection. After that operation, I prognosticated a very limited future for Nels. However, when he attended my wife's funeral at age eighty-seven, he was healthy. At the present age of ninety-one, he is still doing cabinet work.

Undoubtedly, there must be an unknown element of cancer immunity for which there is no known marker. Prior to the advent of chemotherapy, rare cases of spontaneous cures of advanced cancer had been reported in the medical literature. Cancer incidences and deaths are affected by many things, such as preventive and/or prophylactic measures, early diagnostic techniques, and hereditary (DNA) factors. Invasive surgery and chemotherapy have contributed to the remission and cure of this frightening affliction.

Hyperalimentation

ABOUT TWELVE YEARS before my retirement, I became extremely interested in the innovation of hyperalimentation. With the enthusiasm of the dieticians, the interest of Dr. Richard Swenson, a prominent internist, and cooperation of the pharmacy and administration, hyperalimentation was made available at North Memorial Hospital. While the nursing department was very enthusiastic, many of the doctors were not, in spite of attempts to educate them. A frequent question was asked, "Why would someone of your age become so interested in this?" The answer was simple: "I recall many patients from the past who would have lived and some whose recovery would have been precipitously shortened by such administration." Adequate nutrition can be maintained if the proper ratio of nitrogen, carbohydrates, and fat and vitamin requirements are given either by gastrointestinal or intravenous routes. Prior to hyperalimentation, numerous deaths from surgical complications, septic conditions, multiple traumas, and other situations could have been prevented.

To maintain function of the heart, lungs, liver, kidney and brain each person needs a daily basic energy requirement, which is basically, about eight hundred calories. Without any caloric intake, normal liver glycogen will supply about seven hundred calories. After that, body fat will be utilized. Unless there is an increased requirement from catabolic states, such as sepsis or trauma, wherein calories are metabolized from muscle at a very rapid rate, body fat utilization would not apply. Although I used the therapy numerous times, two anecdotal cases will illustrate its value.

A nineteen-year-old girl was seen at North Memorial Hospital in a severely nutritionally depleted state. She had a small bowel obstruction caused by large mesentery fibroid tumors, known as Gardner's

Syndrome. A prominent colorectal surgeon had performed a sub-total colectomy on this patient for colon polyposis. After consulting him during the downhill course, the family was advised to allow her to die either at home or at hospice.

At this point, another M.D., Dr. Kalid Mahmud, a hematologist and oncologist, admitted her and asked for consultation. I maintained intravenous hyperalimentation for two weeks until a positive nitrogen balance was obtained. To relieve her symptoms, surgery was then done, including entero-enterostomy (anastomosis of an obstructed loop of bowel to a normal loop) and resection of several large mesentery fibroidal masses. At surgery, a very small whitish nodule was removed from the surface of the right lobe of the liver. Intravenous nutrition was continued until oral nutrition was adequate.

After recovery, she returned to college. Sadly, however, the white nodule was metastatic colon cancer, and she expired about two years later. Apparently, the resected colon had an undisclosed malignant polyp. Gardner's Syndrome is a genetically transmitted condition in which the individual has multiple colon polyps, along with mesentery fibroidal masses, and cutaneous nodules. The individual would eventually develop cancer of the colon from the polyps.

A second case involved liver pathology. A very good friend, Dr. Roger Anderson, a practicing family physician, admitted a patient with skin stretching abdominal ascites due to alcohol cirrhosis of the liver. The patient was so weak from nutritional depletion that he couldn't get out of bed or to stand. Although a consulted gastroenterologist attempted conservative treatment, the day-to-day and rapidly increasing weakness continued. After Dr. Anderson asked me to see him in consultation, it was obvious continued conservative therapy would only lead to death.

There was only one course for therapy, transfer of the high protein containing ascitic fluid into his blood volume. A system consisting of a one-way valve pocket containing intake and output adapters was utilized. Innovated by a New York surgeon, this technique had been proven effective. A plastic intake tube had to be placed in the peritoneal cavity with the output tube then being inserted into a vein. The valve adapter was buried under his abdominal fascia and skin and the exit tube threaded under the skin up to the neck and into the external and internal jugular vein. Because he was such a poor general anesthetic risk, local anesthesia was utilized while he was wide-awake. Since he had good kidney and heart function, the ascites relented and large volumes of urine were released.

The system was physiologically possible because the abdominal ascitic fluid pressure was greater than that of the intravenous pressure. Infection of the valve pocket would have meant death. Therefore, nutrition and positive nitrogen balance were mandatory. This was easily accomplished by a twenty-four hour drip of one calorie per cc-balanced fluid into the stomach via a small millimeter nasal tube. The gastroenterologist was concerned about hepatic encephalopathy, but my concern was infection prevention of the valve pocket (Hepatic encephalopathy is cellular brain damage due to excessive accumulation of byproducts of protein metabolism).

The dieticians were enthusiastic, and after acceptance by the patient, a twenty-four-hour drip was gradually increased until four thousand calories a day were tolerated. The patient was told it would be continued until he could get out of bed by himself and walk down and back the long hospital corridor. No encephalopathy occurred. Nutritional drip was discontinued after he achieved positive nitrogen balance. He then walked his corridor solo.

By the way, advice was given to him that death might come either by drinking alcohol or by shooting himself with a bullet to the head. Months later, he called our home and informed me that he had just finished walking eighteen holes of golf. He also commented on my bill. "What," I asked, "was it too much?" "No, but the gastroenterologist charged almost the same as you did, even though I was failing rapidly under his care." Since he had played no role, whatsoever in the patient's surgical and nutritional care, I told him to call the gastroenterologist and tell him Doug Adkins feels that the amount was astronomic. He did so. "If you don't *earn* your paycheck, you don't *deserve* it."

The following case is not mine, but is another classic example of the value of hyperalimentation. A highly intelligent minister friend, who lived three months with total intravenous hyperalimentation, related her experience. She lived even after multiple complications, following an initial attempt via a laparoscopic repair of a hiatal hernia. This, in turn, caused lower esophageal mucosal damage from regurgitative gastric juice. Since the blood supply of a large portion of the stomach and the lower esophagus were impaired, a gastrectomy and an esophago-gastrostomy were needed. The surgeon also did a splenectomy.

An esophageal gastrostomy fistula resulted, followed by multiple abdominal abscesses and a wound infection. Permanent sutures produced multiple cutaneous fistulas, which required surgical removal at a later date. A large incisional hernia had to be repaired later at a different hospital and by a different surgeon. The patient, even though alive, had only a portion of her stomach remaining. After her bitter catastrophic experience, she still had esophageal reflux along with limited stomach content. Fortunately, that prominent edifice, the University of Minnesota, which had an excellent nutritional department, saved her life.

In elective cases, adequate nutrition must be started before severe nitrogen depletion has begun. In one such incident, consultation was obtained in a patient who had endured two explorations in order to stop bleeding after a cardiac bypass. Two weeks passed before an attempt was made to start hyperalimentation. It was too late, however, and the patient expired.

Indeed intravenous hyperalimentation is very expensive, but its utilization saves lives and shortens hospitalization.

Close Calls

BECAUSE OF UNINTENTIONAL serious errors, all doctors have close calls. I have been "saved by the bell" several times. Once, I was caring for a forty-year-old patient at North Memorial hospital, who I felt had acute cholecystitis. After several days, I decided if there were no improvement within twenty-four hours, I would do a cholecystectomy. However, on a hunch the day before surgery, I had ordered an electrocardiogram even though the patient had no history of coronary heart disease. The morning of the scheduled surgery, Dr. Frank Martin, who at that time was reading the hospital EKG's, called and told me that the patient had a myocardial infarct. If I had operated, the patient might well have died on the operating table. What might have happened did happen with a surgical colleague who years before had a similar situation. His patient, instead of having acute cholecystitis, had a myocardial infarct and he did not survive.

Another case that might have gone wrong involved a patient referred by Dr. Harley Racer, a highly intelligent family practitioner. The patient was scheduled for a hernia repair. Preoperatively, however, it was noted his blood pressure was unusually high, thereby canceling the operation. Further studies revealed that he had a pheochromocytoma (an adrenal tumor). After proper evaluation and with guidance of an internist, Dr. Racer, the anesthesiologist, and my partner, Dr. Buie, we were able to resect the tumor. It this patient had been taken to the operating room, he would have developed uncontrollable hypertension and most likely would have died on the table.

At another time, because of procrastination, I almost missed a serious condition, namely a partially obstructing carcinoma of the Ampulla of Vater (cancer at the very end of the common bile duct). I had failed to initially evaluate the complete laboratory finding until the time of discharge. The patient's serum bilirubin (bile in the blood) was mildly elevated. A Whipple operation was performed. The patient did well, as I learned from following his case until my retirement. Unlike pancreatic malignancy, cancer of the Ampulla of Vater has at least twenty-five percent, five-year survival rate. Fortunately, this patient surpassed the usual prognosis.

Hazards of Surgery

D R. MAXIENER ONCE reminded me never to be complacent about one's successful cases: "If you do something often, something eventually will go wrong. Furthermore, remember there is no such thing as 'minor surgery.'"

Several cases revealed these truths. One of them was manifested when Dr. Maxiener himself was forced to heed his own advice. When he did a hemroidectomy on an internist's father, excessive bleeding necessitated three returns to the operating room. Another individual expired following a similar operation. The patient bled above the rectal pack, filling the entire colon with blood. Unfortunately, Dr. Maxiener was not notified until the patient went into irreversible shock (Only the referring assistant family doctor had been notified).

In another case involving other doctors, a veteran had surgery (so-called minor surgery) on his toe. After leaving the VA hospital, he had repeated attacks of pulmonary embolism. Since readmission treatment with intravenous heparin failed, he was taken to the OR for ligation of the inferior vena cava. This procedure was to prevent emboli from reaching the lungs. I observed the surgery being performed by the chief resident along with an attending surgeon. During the doctor's dissection and isolation of the inferior vena cava, inadvertent tearing caused massive bleeding. Ligation was finally accomplished but only after multiple transfusions and some very hectic moments.

Although herniorraphy is not minor surgery, serious complications can occur. Three cases illustrate the dichotomy. I recall a mother of two daughters who died from a pulmonary embolism on her way to the discharge desk ten days following Dr. Maxiener's repair of her hernia. Another instance involved me directly. I was called to St. Mary's Hospital from a downtown dinner to see a young priest upon whom I had done a hernia two days earlier. Fortunately, he survived. A post-op appendectomy patient was not so fortunate. This thirty-six-year-old male died suddenly while recovering from surgery for a gangrenous appendix. Present day early ambulation and laparoscopic surgery have significantly reduced this deadly complication.

Abnormal Anatomy

I WAS REMINDED OF a cholecystectomy in which a rare anomaly could have been disastrous. During an operation with Dr. Dick Williams, I first dissected the gallbladder from the fundus down toward the common duct. Then I traced the gallbladder and its cystic duct, which instead of leading to the common duct, lead directly to the duodenum. Further examination revealed that the small common duct had entered the gallbladder and, during the dissection, had been stripped away. The normally forty-five minute operation took three hours because a procedure was performed to allow proper intestinal bile drainage. The family patiently accepted the explanation for the extended surgery.

BOOK VI

Other Facets of my Life

Family Stress

NOT ONLY ARE there challenges and stresses in the hospital but also in the family doctor's home. On May 4, 1944, after I joined Dr. Maxiener, our son Jones was born. Although he was born healthy, his birth permanently scarred his mother's memory because of the horrible painful experience. After twenty-four hours of contractions, she was expecting a hypo for temporary relief; instead, she received pitocin, a powerful medication that initiated violent contractions. At term, she was uncomfortable with Braxton Hicks contractions; therefore, her obstetrician induced her. During several more painful hours, she refused my bedside comfort, apparently not wanting me to see her suffering. Finally birth occurred, relieving the pain. For many years thereafter, however, she had frequent nightmares during which she would wake up screaming. Then, when my arms comforted her, she would quickly fall asleep. Her dreaded fear of another pregnancy obviously affected our love life. I always remember Dad's sagacious saying: "The timetable is not the determining factor in a normal pregnancy; it's the uterus that knows." Remembering this, I was very uneasy when I learned of the induction.

In spite of my wife's apprehension, our daughter Jennifer was born June 5, 1948, just prior to my residency training. Fortunately, her birth was normal. The pediatrician, however, informed us that she had a congenital heart defect, diagnosed by an obvious murmur. We consulted the University of Minnesota's professor of pediatrics who advised us to keep oxygen available at all times and not to allow anyone near her who had a respiratory infection. Above all, we couldn't allow her to cry for any length of time. Also, we needed to administer oxygen if at anytime cyanosis appeared.

She was a well-behaved but very frail infant. We would quickly take her up from the cradle after a few spurts of crying. We rocked her to sleep and took turns holding her during the night. At no time did I observe any sign of heart failure, but it became apparent that she would always require special care during her infancy. I watched her very closely during one short crying spell in which she had no visible evidence of cardiac distress, only facial redness.

One evening while Eudora and her mother were at a Bahai Meeting, I sat down beside my daughter's basket. With a tank of oxygen handy, I waited for bedtime. She started to cry and kick, getting redder and redder with absolutely no evidence of cardiac distress. After a good ten minutes or more, my conscience bothered me so I rectally inserted an eyedropper with a small amount of chlorohydrate and waited. While she continued to cry until she fell asleep, her skin remained normally pink. Returning from the meeting, my wife and her mother were happy to observe the infant sleeping peacefully in her basket. Their demeanor atmosphere quickly changed, however, after I informed them of what I had done. My impression was that even though she had a heart murmur and a congenital defect, it didn't mean that she had incipient heart failure. They agreed to this nightly ritual and finally we allowed her to cry for a reasonable length of time.

As an infant, Jennifer loved to pick up twigs and flowers. She grew up to be healthy with no evidence of myocardial damage. During her teens, a cardiologist evaluated her. We choose the name Jennifer, as she was so dainty. Our stress was compounded when a doctor friend of mine told me, "Appreciate every living day that she will have because I once lost a young son from congenital heart failure." We were thankful that we were diligent in our efforts to sustain her. Fortunately, there were no serious congenital heart defects. She was able to skate, do ballet, and become expert at yoga.

Humiliation

ONE TIME I was humiliated in front of my peers by an arrogant doctor. While a group of the staff doctors was enjoying coffee in the small doctors' room adjacent to the OR, a family physician entered and told me that one of his associates had admitted a patient with GI bleeding. He said it was a patient upon whom I had previously done a gastric resection for peptic ulcer hemorrhage. I hesitated, but before I left, I saw the reaction in the crowded room. The opportunist surgeon slapped the adjoining table, and in a loud voice repeatedly said, "Never, but never have I had a recurring bleeding in any patient upon whom I have performed a gastric resection for peptic ulcer hemorrhage." I left for the patient's floor in order to first review the chart. Not surprised, I saw the patient wasn't mine, but belonged to the orator. With chart in hand, I rushed down to the room in order to present the error to the appropriate owner. I was disappointed to find everyone had departed except the vociferous surgeon. After notification his only response, with not an iota of humility, was, "Oh!"

Other unpleasant situations at this same hospital involved the hospital administrator and the physicians as well. One beautiful afternoon my outdoor activity was interrupted when my wife called me: "Hurry; there is an emergency at North Memorial hospital." The message was, "Doug, I have a child in the ER with a ruptured spleen. Will you come? The covering surgeon refuses to respond." I replied, "I will leave immediately." To vent my displeasure, I drove by the administrator's home where he was outside entertaining guests. I called him over to my car window and with a loud high octave voice said, "I am on my way to operate on a child who has a ruptured spleen. Your powerful intimidating doctor, who was covering, refuses to come." I added, "Vance, he could shit in your operative suite and you wouldn't say a word." While

I was unable to preserve the spleen, the abdomen containing over one-third total blood volume was aspirated. The child survived.

A few days later the administrator, Mr. DeMong, called me into his office and reprimanded me, saying that I had insulted his guests, especially Miss Fremming, his long-standing girlfriend. I don't remember his inquiring about the child's welfare. This conversation took place on Monday, compounding my unpleasant encounter the day before. On that same day, while making rounds, I met the family physician who was the Saturday emergency caller. While he was doing charting, I suggested that the refusal of the surgeon to obligate his duty should be reported to his partners. His only comment: "Doug, thanks for coming." With more affirmation, I repeated the suggestion. Again, without looking up from the desk he said, "Thanks for coming."

I had two other encounters with the aforementioned administrator. One fall I had been hospitalized with a badly shattered right femoral and hip fracture, which I had suffered in a horseback riding accident. A day after my long reparative operation, a congenial and gourmet friend, Dr. Fred Holzaphel, visited me. This amicable friend, who took great enjoyment in preparing food and drinks, left a cooler on the floor at the left of my bedside. Shortly after, the administrator's nurse, Miss Fremming, walked in, pointed at the cooler and condescendingly asked me, "What is that for? What's in it?" I said, "I don't know. You know Freddie Holzaphel. He brought it in." She turned and exited. I had known Miss Fremming for many years, even at one time having removed her appendix. She had been a probie nurse at the Old Asbury Hospital.

Having so much pain, I was totally unable to turn without help. It wasn't long before Vance DeMong appeared at the foot of the bed. Same question: "What's that cooler doing here? What's in it?" My answer to him was the same. With that, he pointed his finger at me and emphatically said, "Just because you are a doctor, don't think you can expect any special treatment." Being vehemently opposed to alcohol, he apparently thought the cooler contained booze.

Neither he nor Fremming ever visited again. Revenge was their desire. When I was being discharged to Fairview Hospital, in order to obtain more specific physical therapy, such as swimming pool exercises, I asked one of the many friendly nurses to please deliver the unopened cooler to Miss Fremming's office. Turnabout is fair play.

Mr. DeMong had been a diligent and energetic administrator. He prevailed against many odds, rapidly bringing the fledging hospital into an exemplary modern unit. At its incipiency, it was considered a "second rate" health center. His endeavors were well recognized and during the hospital ascent, an auditorium utilized for credit teaching, was named after him.

My next encounter with Mr. DeMong took place after the board of directors asked him to either retire amiably or be fired. Prior to that, an ad hoc committee of staff doctors had initiated legal advice in order to have DeMong's administrative role terminated. He had become incompetent not because of age but because of drug abuse.

During a party for North Memorial personnel who had had twenty-five years of service, I went up to him to shower a few accolades for his appreciated past service. Instead of accepting my overture, he heaped a torrent of verbal abuse about the ad hoc committee of which I was a member. Not only was he angry with me personally but irate at the entire committee. He threatened hospital litigation, but after a financial settlement, he resigned. Prior to his death from cancer, his bitterness modified.

Once during my residency I became aware of medical patronizing, which gave me a peek into the corporate atmosphere. Dr. Hay graciously allowed me to have several days off in order to earn some extra dollars. I was paid to be the attending doctor on an exclusive pheasant hunting train expedition to Pierre, South Dakota. Each year the sixty-year-old president of the M & L Railroad invited corporate CEO's to accompany him on a private train. Since some of them were elderly, he wanted medical coverage available. Dr. Lynch, a family practitioner asked me to fill in.

Early in the morning of the second day of the guided hunt, I was abruptly awakened. Someone shouted, "Hurry and get up, the president is ill." Grabbing my black bag, I ran down the aisle to the president's private car. The Asbury hospital administrator was kind enough to allow me to borrow sufficient supplies to take care of most emergencies. The diagnosis, after examination of the relaxed president, was flu syndrome as he had a low-grade fever, stuffy nose, mild head and body aches. I reassured the emotional, upset attending officials that his condition was not serious and he would be okay with rest, fluids and aspirin. Completely ignoring my advice, they rushed around, making

long-distanced phone calls, insisting the patient immediately should
be returned to Minneapolis. So, the president, his personal cook, and
I traveled back to Minneapolis in his private train section. During the
return trip, I stayed at his bedside. Even though he was the president,
he suddenly scoffed at the utter confusion and the decision to leave the
hunting party. Later, knowing that he was upset about the departure
and his illness, I administered a hypodermic injection of fifty milligrams
of Demerol. When he relaxed, he went into a long discussion about his
wonderful and beautiful wife. Then he asked me to hand him his pants
that were hanging on a door hook. He removed a new fifty-dollar bill
and complimented me for my care. (The fifty dollars were in addition
to the daily doctor fee of the same amount.) After he had fallen asleep,
I had a good visit with his friendly, admiring, African-American chef,
who described some of the president's favorite foods.

In the early morning a few moments after the train had stopped, I
was shocked when a tall young blond woman wrapped in a leopard fur
coat came dashing down the aisle. She was followed by a plodding and
puffy fat man carrying a black bag. I had expectations of the president's
wife being a sophisticated gray haired lady. She rushed into the state-
room, crying out, "Darling, darling how are you?" His answer, "I am
fine, this young doctor took good care of me." She looked at me and
while patting my cheek, said, "Thank you. That's what doctors are for,
aren't they?" By that time, the flushed fat German internist had reached
us. I attempted to discuss my examination and treatment to him, but
he completely ignored me. I grabbed my equipment and made a hasty
exit. When I got home, I told Eudora; "In no way do I want to take
care of the corporate realm. The patronization of that doctor sickened
me."

Success and Failures

MOST PHYSICIANS ARE reinforced when their actions and deeds produce success in critical situations. This was true of me. As were the Dorn parents, I was extremely pleased as a participant in a life-saving measure for their six-year-old son, Jim. The incident took place when they were visiting Eudora's sister and husband on their farm one hundred fifty miles southwest of Minneapolis. When my wife and I arrived, I was immediately rushed into the bedroom where the young child was feverish and flushed with complaints of headaches. A very quick initial examination revealed a "stiff neck." I immediately called North Memorial emergency room and informed them that I would be there as soon as possible with a critical child suffering from spinal meningitis. When I arrived, in record time, a spinal tap confirmed my diagnosis. Antibiotic therapy produced rapid and uncomplicated recovery. Jim grew up to own a very successful automobile business.

Another time I saved a young man from the operating room for a wrong diagnosis. He came to our office complaining of abdominal pain. His physical examination was negative as well as his white blood count; however, when he was asked if he had any exposure to lead, he said, "Yes, I work in a battery manufacturing plant." Diagnosis: lead poisoning. This was confirmed in the laboratory by blood smears that revealed stippling of the red cells.

In another case, after initiating diagnosis, I recommended hospitalization for a teenager who then required special treatment. Dr. Maxiener sent me on a house call to see a young girl who had severe flu-like symptoms. Not only was she complaining of aches and pains but also of weakness of her limbs and mild difficulty breathing. Physical examination was essentially negative except for a slight weakness of her extremities and a mild rigidity of her neck. She was immediately hospitalized with a diagnosis of Guilland-Barre Disease (a viral disease simulating poliomyelitis). A neurologist was called who confirmed the diagnosis. Shortly after admission, she developed respiratory distress. She was quickly transported to the University Hospital, where she was placed in an iron lung. A long period of hospitalization preceded her recovery.

Along with successes, there are haunting deaths, some of which were personal failures: a nurse's mother's death after multiple operations for a transected duodenum, a male patient who died from a crushing blow to the abdomen and who suffered superior mesentery artery trauma plus duodenal and pancreatic trauma, and a fifty-year-old man who expired from pancreatitis most likely compounded by my sphincterotomy of sphincter of Oddi (incision of the sphincter at the end of the common duct). There were other deaths from intestinal surgery. The first patient died from the failure of the gastroenerostomy to function even after re-exploration. The other patient died following a right colectomy—probably from complications of poor nutrition.

I was responsible for other deaths as well. A patient died from a small bowel torsion following a Whipple operation for a small cancer at the head of the pancreas. Another patient died during the night after an eight-hour operation for removal of a cancer of the hepatic duct. Yet another expired from a pulmonary embolism following an appendectomy for gangrenous appendix. (This was before very early ambulation). In another case, an obese person succumbed suddenly in the intensive care unit from respiratory failure. She died the first post-operative night, following surgery for a large malignant ovarian cyst. Another patient expired after total gastrectomy. Prior to the innovation of vascular surgery, a patient referred by Dr. Bernie Nauth, died on the table due to a ruptured abdominal aneurysm.

Sad Moments

WHILE IN SURGICAL practice, a doctor will inevitably face sad moments. After I had performed breast surgery on a lovely forty-five-year-old Italian wife, she was admitted to hospice for terminal care. As I stopped by to say hello, she took my hand, looked at me and said, "I am not doing very well, am I?" and with that, she expired.

Several other experiences saddened me. One involved a young student who died from multiple traumas: severe head injury, a fractured leg, and internal injuries. This tragedy occurred just after another tragedy. His father, an attorney, had been killed in a plane crash while he was on a fishing trip. It was difficult to inform the family that their fifty-year-old father and husband had died from pancreatitis.

Just as devastating was telling parents of the death of a daughter who had massive liver rupture. Painful also, it was for me to inform the parents that their nine-year-old boy had a cardiac arrest. It occurred during the drainage of large thigh abscess, which had resulted from a complication of a previous bone operation by an orthopedic surgeon. Then I will always remember the cries of a mother whose boy had committed suicide.

More poignantly, during the first year of my apprenticeship with Dr. Maxiener, I was a witness and neophyte participant in a profound parental tragedy. I am now convinced it could have been averted. A child with a ruptured kidney was admitted to the old Asbury Hospital. The parents had requested Dr. Maxiener, so I received the initial call. Even though he was on the golf course, I informed him this child was in a very serious condition. Unbelievably, he said he would come only after he had finished the final few holes. Unfortunately, by the time of his arrival it was too late. The child expired. The mother threw her arms around me and pleaded, "Save my child, save my child!" Being young and inexperienced, I was helpless. Trauma experience came years later, but time didn't absolve that memory.

All members of the medical profession occasionally have to meet these emotional burdens. When a doctor accepts his career, he needs to be aware of this task. Now days hospices have transferred some of the responsibility in care of the dying. Those caring individuals deserve ultimate praise.

Self Confidence and Ego

EGO PLAYS A role in one's journey of life regardless of avocation. Abundance of self-confidence, however, may elicit retribution. Surgeons for example, with self-confidence will handle difficult procedures without hesitation. Those with over confidence, those with limited training and experience, may find themselves in a difficult situation. Some illustrations follow:

An out of town family practitioner phoned me, stating, "I have a patient on the operating table who has appendicitis, but I can't find the appendix. What should I do?" Answer: "Close the incision and administer antibiotics. He has a retrocecal appendix. Call me if he doesn't improve." He improved and six weeks later I removed his retrocecal appendix.

On another occasion, the doctor who had some limited training summoned me to the OR. He had made a pre-operative diagnosis of acute appendicitis. The appendix was normal but the symptoms were caused by sigmoid diverticulitis.

The goal of all specialties of course, is to obtain the American Board Certification. To achieve this goal, written and oral examinations are given to test training requirements. The oral examination is usually given by various university department heads that have had intensive surgical experience. The preparation for general surgery examination, a basic knowledge of other surgery specialties, is necessary, such as neurosurgery, plastic and orthopedics.

Because of arrogance, a surgical resident once failed his first oral examination. He was one of Dr. Owen Wagensteen's "boys" who was being groomed by the world-renowned surgeon to become head of surgery at another university. One basic orthopedic question he was asked was, "How do you treat an eight-year-old-boy's femoral shaft fracture?" The resident's answer: "I don't do fractures." Dr. Wagensteen called one of his friends on the examining board and asked, "Why are you doing that to one of my staff?" Six months later, the resident did pass his oral examination.

Some doctors maintain their ego by surreptitious methods. My wife told me of one such situation. She worked ten to twelve hours a day as a laboratory technician and typist for a prominent and busy Minneapolis Obstetrician and Gynecologist. While the senior partner saw his patients on schedule, his junior partner would allow his patients to "pile up" before he would enter the waiting room to summon the first patient. He once surprisingly admitted that he wanted to impress his patients about his busy schedule. Because he was ashamed of his elderly Norwegian father, he never allowed him to "dawdle" in the waiting room.

After years of experience, a doctor's arrogance and ego are often replaced by humility.

Grateful Patients

DURING THEIR CAREERS, all physicians have had the satisfaction of having grateful patients. These appreciations often reinforce their decision to continue the interplay of medicine. It may boost one's ego. A few anecdotal cases of appreciation follow:

On one patient, I was able to excise a one-centimeter squamous cell cancer from the glans penis of a forty-year-old patient. Fortunately, he had an unusually large appendage.

A sixty-year-old widow had a very large villous adenoma of the rectum, which was successfully removed via the anus, thus negating an abdominal-perineal resection and colostomy. Prior to surgery, I had prepared her for the possibility of that extensive resection. During follow-up examinations, she repeatedly expressed her gratitude.

Another example was with the aforementioned young Butch Bakken, who was forever thankful that his forearm was saved. My expertise, which saved him from having a prosthesis, enabled him to continue with his sports.

Likewise, my friends the Dorn family felt that their son Jim fully recovered from the spinal meningitis only because of the wild emergency ride to the hospital.

The most memorable expression of thanks took place in a dramatic way. While I was making rounds at Fairview Hospital, I met an elderly patient whose ileo-vaginal fistula I had repaired. When she saw me, she fell on her knees in the corridor, wrapped her arms around my legs, and thanked me for relief from the very painful perineum. I had admitted this patient from a nursing home where I found her moaning, all curled up in bed. She was desperate to obtain even mild relief from an extremely painful red excoriating rash over her entire perineum caused by the outpouring fecal like fluid via the fistula. Her perineum was the mirror image of that of a baboon. This complication had followed colon surgery. I was happy to assume the treatment of this patient after the notified surgeon had release her care to me. Her reaction at the time surprised me. The touching scene later brought me to tears.

Prior to retiring, I made a diagnosis that probably prevented permanent multi-limb paralysis. I had done a right femoral artery implant graft with my partner Dr. Woyda's guidance. The patient complained of progressive weakness of his legs. Since examination revealed no evidence of arterial insufficiency, he was immediately referred to a neurologist and admitted on his service. While I was making rounds the next day, I stopped in to just say hello. Since admission, he had become so weak he was unable to stand up without support. He also stated that his upper extremities were extremely weak. The IV stand was nearby. He was about to receive ACTH—adrenal cortical thyroid hormone. All of a sudden, it struck me: A Scandinavian with blue eyes, a smooth tongue and marked muscle weakness added up to presumptive diagnosis of Pernicious Anemia. Laboratory studies immediately confirmed it. Incidentally, I had checked the chart and his hemoglobin was within normal limits. When vitamin B was initiated, rapid improvement began. We didn't do family practice, but the patient insisted that we follow him and administer the vitamin B-12.

Another patient, Nels Olson, has been appreciative through all his fifty-seven years of recovery. He survived surgery of a malignant melanoma on his back along with axillary node dissection for extensive lymph node metastases.

Sometimes patients need reassuring to erase their doubts. A referring physician scheduled a gastric resection on an elderly lady whose pre-operative x-ray diagnosis was probable cancer of the stomach. The patient was initially irate when she was told her condition was benign. She felt the surgery was unnecessary and the fee unreasonable. She was told if it had been cancer, surgery could not have assured her of one hundred per cent cure. After a lengthy office visit, she accepted my sincere explanation. She then seem amiable to the limited fees.

There are times in a doctor's career when the Hippocratic oath becomes paradoxic. The decision may bode well for the patient or it may not. On one occasion I operated on a Catholic mother who had an early ectopic pregnancy in the mid-portion of the right fallopian tube. (The left fallopian tube was pathologically defective.) A decision had to be made to either remove the tube, causing permanent sterility or to repair the tube for future pregnancies. When I consulted the husband about the tube procedures, his answer was, "use your judgment. I have confidence in you." I went back to the operating table and repaired the tube. Months later she had a successful pregnancy, thus avoiding another ectopic pregnancy. Not only were the parents delighted with the outcome but I also was so pleased that I published the case in a medical journal.

Speaking Out: Better to Keep One's Mouth Shut

A<small>T TIMES, IT</small> may be prudent not to voice an opinion, just remain acquiescent. I didn't always follow that motto. My words have sometimes caused professional irritation.

Once I operated on a patient with duodenal obstruction caused by massive retroperitoneal hemorrhage, a complication from Coumadin (blood coagulant depressant). I told the patient that while Coumadin was an excellent drug, it was dangerous without careful monitoring. He related this warning to the referring family physician who in turn called me with a wrathful reprimand. Needless to say, that ended any further referrals. Just prior to that incident, I had been reading about Coumadin complications. I was impressed by the case of a bilateral adrenal gland hemorrhage and impairment producing permanent Addison's disease. (This disease is marked by deficient secretion of an adrenal cortical hormone and characterized by extreme weakness, weight loss and hypotension, gastrointestinal problems, and brownish pigmentation of skin and mucus membrane.)

Another incident when I should have kept my mouth shut was at Fairview Hospital, where I had been on the staff for only a short time. During a late fall staff meeting, discussion was held relative to the usual nurses' Christmas gifts, the yearly giving of poinsettia plants for each nursing desk. Sheepishly, I volunteered that a yearly nurses' fund could be utilized during an emergency nurse's financial situation. There was complete silence. Voting was unanimous (except for me) to continue with the plant supply.

Although there was no retribution in the next incidents, I was definitely vulnerable. As I stated earlier, the Hennepin County Medical

Society had an ad hoc committee consisting of doctors representing the various specialties. The purpose of this group was to review case reports (doctors' names blotted out) in which the patient or the patient's insurance company considered the charge unreasonable. After the review, we would accept the charge or agree that it was unreasonable. In most cases, the committee would ask for more information. While having coffee prior to the meeting, I directed a question to a plastic surgeon. "We are all here on a voluntary basis in order to see reasonable parity in fees. Also, we chose medicine as our avocation in order to be of some service as well as being assured of a comfortable living. Something, however, disturbs me. I cannot understand why you charge more to make a breast smaller or larger than surgeons do for life saving cancer breast surgery." His face flushed—I received no response. I still don't understand, but probably because of high malpractice insurance.

At one meeting, it would have been better to have kept my mouth shut. At that time, I was secretary of the Minneapolis Surgical Society, which consisted of doctors who either had their surgical boards or were members of the American College of Surgeons. It was apparent to me that there was considerable variation in surgical fees. Since all members were trained, I suggested, as I had before, that we should meet and agree on set fees for common surgical procedures, along with a reasonable standard deviation. There was no discussion—just silence. However, since apparently no one agreed with me, my speaking out was impudent.

Errors of Judgment

SOMETIMES ERRORS OF judgment occur causing unnecessary surgery. Once when I operated on a patient with carcinoma of the stomach, I failed to review the admitting chest film. Had I checked the x-ray, I obviously would not have operated. The x-ray revealed pulmonary metastases. Since at that, time radiologists were not full-time at the hospital, the admitting films were reviewed many hours after hospital admission.

Moreover, I once was guilty of making a mistake with a colleague. At St. Mary's Hospital, Dr. John Clarke admitted one of his patients with abdominal pain and marked abdominal distension. My abdominal exploration was negative. He had a prolonged post-operative ileus that required nasal suction. Chest film revealed a distinct ball of pneumonia in the right lung, apparently the cause of his symptoms.

Other times I missed or refused the pathologist's diagnosis. A male jaundiced patient was explored with a pre-operative diagnosis of a common duct obstruction. His jaundice was caused by Thorazine, a depressant drug. I had failed to uncover this in the pre-operative valuation. Fortunately, he recovered from an unnecessary operation.

More seriously, I was responsible for the death of a middle-aged man who died because of my refusal to accept Dr. Semba's biopsy diagnosis of benign fibrosis. I resected a massive duodenal non-malignant obstructive mass, which was simply caused by the drug Sansert. This drug, which caused extensive fibroidal proliferation, was being used for treatment of migraine headaches.

BOOK VII

Some Later Epiphanies

A Tribute to Nurses

WITH THE EXCEPTION of my high school years, I have been associated with nurses from my childhood to age sixty-five. That relationship has taught me what important participants they are in the care of the sick. Also, what a major adjunct they are to the doctors. Without them, how could we as physicians perform effectively? Fortunately, they have risen from emptying bedpans, washing floors and windows, and making beds to a much higher status. Some now have master's and Ph.D. degrees. This new respect has elevated them from hard work and low pay to highly qualified and respected positions.

My Wife, Eudora

I HAD KNOWN MY beloved and beautiful Swedish Eudora since I was four. I remember our sitting on a rock near Bush's garage on a beautiful early summer evening. There, at age eight, I asked her to marry me. Fourteen years later, we signed the contract. From the beginning of our marriage in 1939, she reinforced my desire to obtain credited training and willingly accepted the financial hardships that would follow. She tolerated the enumerable interruptions of home phone calls, missed meal times, and holiday interferences. Eudora kept her mind active by voluminous reading of philosophy, sociology, religion and mythology. She twice read Darwin's *Origin of the Species*. She took many correspondence courses from the University of Minnesota, receiving A's in all of them. Later she gave many talks, presented several papers, and wrote two books, including some inspired by the Bahai faith. Others were about women's rights. While she was not a feminist, she believed strongly in the equality of women.

From early life, she had been deprived of religion due to her father's refusal for his children to attend religious services. She investigated and attended various ministries. At age thirty-five, she learned of the Bahai Faith; after *intensive* investigation, she declared herself a Bahai.

Three other talents could have been careers. She had an operatic voice, specializing in German Lieder. She also was an accomplished violinist. Along with her music, she developed an interest in cooking. Heaps of recipes were scattered about the house. With her sense of humor, she wrote a whimsical book about gourmet cooking.

Above all, she was a very devoted mother, instilling in our two children the habit of cleanliness, love of music, fondness for good food, and respect for all mankind without prejudice. These endeavors were achieved in spite of living for many years with severe back pain, caused by a degenerated spine. In 2001, our marriage of sixty-five years ended when she died from an unexpected heart attack. She was eighty-five years old.

Retirement

REGARDLESS OF AVOCATION, there comes a time when the shingle has to be taken down and a sign put up "Closed for Good—Leaving for Greener Pastures." Within the medical profession, the incipiency of retirement is manifold; namely, "fed up," "too much interference from direct patient care," "health," "sufficient pecuniary reasons," "other things to do," and unfortunately, "license seizure because of substance abuse or incompetence."

In the years prior to the sixties, rarely did we hear discussion about retirement. In recent years, this is a frequent subject among doctors. "How much do you need?" "What are you going to do?" "Where can I be of value?" "What hobbies do you have?"

In 1956, one busy family doctor said he had two million dollars saved. With those savings, he could retire, but he loved his practice so much he wouldn't quit. Later, at age sixty-five he did retire. He trained and specialized in physical therapy.

After I had retired, an otolaryngologist friend told me he had over two million dollars. He asked me, "Will that be sufficient for retirement?" My monetary reserve being extremely short of that amount, I quickly affirmed his question.

Some medical groups have mandatory age retirements. At the Mayo Clinic, the age is sixty-five. Sometimes, at any age, doctors may be forced to quit due to incompetence. One such doctor was a very well known and respected Minneapolis orthopedic surgeon. When his privileges were removed because of incompetence, he became inflamed. He threatened tort proceedings and even tried soliciting support from his peers.

I choose retirement at age sixty-five. A self-critic, I was confident of my own ability. I feared waiting for the day when the surgical committee would inform me that my major surgery privileges would be removed. I was tired also of fulfilling my "call schedule."

When you are a partner, it is your duty to whole-heartedly contribute to that role. Most important of all, I wanted my exit at a time when I could retain respect and friendship with my full partners, Drs. Woyda, Buie and Nemanich. Since then some of my peers have said, "Doug, you retired too early." "No, I didn't," was my reply. "I miss surgery, but I don't regret leaving it."

As I sit here recalling my past, an image symbolizing my rich life, a simple utilitarian vial integral part of me is the doctor's bag. When I was five-years-old, I was fascinated by the contents of my father's bag, namely its medicinal smell, various bottles, kits and mysterious instruments. Because of the time I spent with him in his office, or on numerous calls when I went with him, some of the "country doctor" glided onto me. His doctor bag was his constant companion, and even though at times his treatment was to no avail, his presence with his bag exuded confidence.

I always looked forward to the day when I would have a bag as an emblem of my profession. It was necessary to own one when I made calls for Dr. Maxiener. Also, during my surgical residency, I supplemented my meager monthly income by making five-dollar house calls during off times at my residency. Now as I enter my nonagenarian years, the memory of that bag (actually, I had two of them) occupies my thoughts. At one time, a noble item, now it is simply a non-sentimental container for my son's fishing gear. Such are the vicissitudes of life.

With oil painting

Author with painting of his wife, Eudora, in Minnesota

Son, Dr. Jones Adkins

Author fishing

Author fishing

Retiring doctor expresses thanks

To all of you:

January 13, 1982—The North Memorial Tea was a day that I will always remember and cherish. I sincerely express my heartfelt thanks.

I have watched the metamorphosis of North Memorial from an embryo, to a fledgling and into a full structured unit that is now called a medical center. During this rapid transition, I have had the golden opportunity to be associated with an excellent expanding hospital staff consisting of the "attendings" and the hospital personnel. It is now an exemplary unit.

Time and space does not permit an eclectic selection other than to emphasize that an important aspect of any successful organization is, in part, measured by its continuing research and *education*. Also, success fails unless there is an inner spirit of warmth and cooperation.

We must always remind ourselves, regardless of how important or unimportant one might feel, that the primal reason of the entire unit is to serve and benefit the pa-

C. D. Adkins, MD, recently traded hats, from the surgical cap he has worn for over 25 years as a surgeon on the North Memorial Medical Staff, to a Vikings cap given to him at his retirement party on January 13, 1982.

tient and not vice versa. Each individual is a link in this chain of health care, and consequently, each link is of equal importance.

Again, I am humbly grateful to have had the opportunity to have been associated with all of you.

Hasta Luego,

Dr. Adkins

Author as chief of staff at North Memorial Hospital in Minneapolis.

Testimonials

Doug Adkins has seen many changes in medicine from accompanying his father, a horse and buggy doctor in northern Minnesota to practicing surgery in a major metropolitan hospital and trauma center in Minneapolis. He is eminently qualified to chronicle his experiences and observations as a superior surgeon and physician. Because of the diversity of his training, the depth of his knowledge, his exceptional skills, and his forthright attitude, he was held in high esteem by his colleges.

Surgically he utilized flawless, gentle techniques with the eye and touch of an artist. Patients benefited considerably from this combination.

I appreciated his strict adherence to the Code of Medical Ethics, and it is my good fortune to call him my partner, mentor, and close friend for forty-seven years.

Louis "Bud" Buie

Dear Doug:

As I reflect on my surgical training and career, I count you as one of my significant mentors in the practice of surgery.

As a young surgeon coming into practice in 1972, some 35 years ago, I certainly appreciated the skill, knowledge and surgical judgment you displayed on a day-to-day basis in our surgical practice.

We had quite a few challenging cases that we worked on together and your experience and support was very helpful. Not only were you a great surgeon technically but you also had a wonderful relationship with your patients. You truly were a patient advocate for some people who needed additional help to get through their surgical procedure.

In addition to all your other attributes, I remember and admire

221

your interest in an advocacy for nutritional support of the surgical patient. You were a real pioneer in the area at North Memorial, and in the entire metro area, and now nutritional support of the surgical patient is a standard of care for all of our surgical patients.

Doug, I do treasure the memories of their early years in the practice of surgery with you, Bud and Bill. They were busy days and we helped a lot of people.

Best regards,
Dr. George J. Nemanich, M.D.

In July 1952, I began my formal practice of medicine in Watertown, Minnesota, population 750. The hospital was a converted two-story family home with the OR the upstairs bedroom. It was equipped with an OR table and all the necessary accompanying equipment, albeit rather sparse.

Anesthesia was administered either by me or the surgeon as drip ether, spinal or local infiltration. We were ale to do multiple types of surgery with good RN assistance.

Shortly after my start, I met Dr. C.D. Adkins, who was just beginning his private surgical practice. I had assisted him on several occasions in Minneapolis at the major hospitals and was quite impressed with his surgical skills and medical demeanor. He showed great respect for human tissue and treated it accordingly, "gently with care." I was equally impressed by his use of local anesthesia. These skills were first used for me, only after my first month in practice, when I asked him to consult and possibly operate on a 2-year-old girl with a possible perforated appendix. Since this child had been symptomatic for less than one and one-half hours, the diagnosis was questioned by Dr. Adkins. As I was my own laboratory, I found the WBC to be above 20,000 with 90% PMN. Dr. Adkins reluctantly drove the 40 miles to see this patient, all the time doubting the surgical need. However, after seeing the patient, he concurred and under ether anesthesia, we operated and removed a gangrenous appendix. The youngster had a total uneventful recovery.

Dr. A spent many visits at the Watertown hospital performing appendectomies, hernias, gall bladders and mastectomies, all under either local or spinal anesthesia. There was never a post-op complication.

Later, I moved to a larger, yet still quite small community hospital with better equipment and more RN assistance. Here Dr. A performed multiple surgical procedures under local, general and spinal anesthesia.

One patient in particular, Ms. Arnold, had refused surgery for a large ovarian cysts. But because the tumor had finally severally compromised her breathing due to pressure on the diaphragm, she consented to the surgery. Under local anesthesia we removed a 28-pound ovarian cyst. This lady also had a totally benign recovery.

Over the next 16-17 years, Dr. A performed many surgical procedures: bowel resections, gastric resections, thyroidectomies—all with no post-op complications. I was continually impressed by his gentle, almost delicate handling of human tissue, as if he were holding a demitasse coffee cup, protecting the unaffected bowel without harm our injury. He continued to use only the finest number suture possible: 5-0, 4-0.

One anecdote bears repeating. Dr. A had a hobby farm on which he planted corn and harvested hay, about 25 acres as I remember. Dr. A had completed a bowel resection for cancer of the colon on a Mr. Lafe Varner, a true Swede from the old country—accent and all. Mr. Varner was seen for a six-week post-op check when Dr. Adkins entered the room commenting about his fatigue from raking and baling hay. Mr. Varner's startled reply, with all sincerity, "Doc, I have all kinds of farmer friends who would not have charged me anywhere what you did for my surgery." Needless to say, Dr. A has been reminded several times of this incident over the years.

Dr. A gave me the supreme compliment by accepting almost without question my pre-op diagnoses and the allowing me to continue all post-op care. Dr. A was not an itinerant surgeon the old sense of the word. As our area was a heavy farming community, it was important if at all possible for the patient to be cared for close to the home. Dr. A fully understood this and treated the patient in these small hospitals when it would have been easier for him to transfer the patient to the larger hospital. However, there was never a compromise of care.

In all those years, 1952 to 1968, working in very primitive settings (certainly by today's standards), I am unable to recall losing a single patient or having a surgical post-op complication.

Time will not allow details of the varied procedures handled expertly over the years by Dr. A in those small rural hospitals.

Suffice it to say, few surgeons would have performed so expertly or so willingly in those times and places of need. Many patients and I share a large debt of gratitude for Dr. A.

Dr. John Clarke, M.D.

The able Dr. Willian Woyda joined Dr. Buie and me as a partner in 1965.

Tony Brand
215 632 740

Printed in the United States
139397LV00003B/132/P